Business Intelligence

Business Intelligence

Making Decisions Through Data Analytics

Jerzy Surma

translated by

Magdalena Górniakowska and Peter Gee

Business Intelligence: Making Decisions Through Data Analytics
Copyright © Business Expert Press, LLC, 2011.

First published in 2011 by
Business Expert Press, LLC
222 East 46th Street, New York, NY 10017
www.businessexpertpress.com

ISBN-13: 978-1-60649-185-0 (paperback)
ISBN-13: 978-1-60649-186-7 (e-book)

10.4128/9781606491867

A publication in the Business Expert Press Small Business Management and Entrepreneurship collection

Collection ISSN: 2150-9611 (print)
Collection ISSN: 2150-9646 (electronic)

Cover design by Jonathan Pennell
Interior design by Scribe Inc.

First edition: February 2011.

10 9 8 7 6 5 4 3 2 1

Printed in Taiwan

Abstract

This book is about using business intelligence as a management information system for supporting managerial decision making. It concentrates mainly on practical business issues and demonstrates how to apply data warehousing and data analytics to support decision making. This book progresses through a logical sequence, starting with data model infrastructure, then data preparation, followed by data analysis, integration, knowledge discovery, and finally the actual use of discovered knowledge. All examples are based on the newest achievements in business intelligence (BI). Finally, this book outlines an overview of a methodology that takes into account the complexity of developing applications in an integrated BI environment.

Keywords

competing on analytics, online analytical processing, data warehouse, information management, business process monitoring, data mining, customer intelligence, value-based management

Contents

Introduction

Quid est Veritas?

—John 18:38

At present, information technology (IT) is applied in so many business fields that it seems to be the "sine qua non" of development in the modern economy. It is fascinating that IT appeared in areas directly connected with the intellectual achievements of human beings. More surprisingly, it all happened when the most optimistic of research projects, artificial intelligence, spectacularly collapsed. The realistic approach, in which a computer program is designed not to replace a man but to support his activities based on intelligence, turned out to be extremely fruitful and was successfully employed in the business world. A few years later, this field was called business intelligence (BI), as it refers to the implementation of IT systems, which simulate intelligent behavior, to support business decisions.

This book is an account of my long-standing experience in building solutions that support intelligent systems in terms of both research and real business applications. When it comes to research, it all began during my studies at the Wroclaw Technical University, where at the Institute of Control Systems in the late 1980s the theory of expert systems was being formed. This was a turbulent yet creative moment in Poland's history—that is, a few years before the fall of the communism—and as a student I was lucky enough to meet on my road eminent professors and other people committed to an independent Poland. Let me mention my outstanding mathematics professors Hanna Pidek-Lopuszanska, Andrzej Kisielewicz, Roman Rozanski, and Andrzej Zarach, who as heirs of the Lwow-Warsaw school of logic shared this spirit with me.

Finally, I wrote my PhD dissertation on the application of expert systems in management, which I defended at the Wroclaw University of Economics, where one of the first teams dealing with the business aspects of artificial intelligence was created. Later, I spent a few years doing research into data-mining methods and case-based reasoning in business in research institutes in France and Belgium. After returning to Poland, I worked for international consulting firms and I was in charge of a large number of BI implementations in leading Polish enterprises. Currently, I am a research worker at the Collegium of Business Administration at the Warsaw School of Economics and the director of postgraduate BI studies. In this book I give my original presentation of the subject. I have selected the most significant aspects and I have presented them in the context of real business applications and their real influence on the enhancement of a company's value.

In the first chapter the history of BI is presented, the terms are defined, and the representative applications in business are reviewed. The second chapter describes a warehouse, which is an elementary component of BI systems. I am convinced that insight into the technological dimension translates into a better understanding of both the limitations of those systems and business owners' realistic expectations. The third chapter introduces analytical data mining and describes basic analytical operations with a simple example. Section 3.1 deals with managerial information and its application in various areas in enterprise. The use of BI tools in the management of business processes and a company's strategy by means of a balanced scorecard are discussed separately. The subsequent section, 3.2, is devoted to the problem of strategic information management, or the analysis of information in an enterprise environment, which influences the strategic development of a given company. The whole of the fourth chapter deals with data exploration. Four classic tasks are discussed at length: classification, estimation, discovery of association rules, and cluster analysis. All of these are conducted by means of advanced data analysis algorithms. Limitations of data exploration methods are analyzed in detail, and standard applications are reviewed. The fifth chapter presents issues connected with the analysis of personal data and its application in direct marketing. It also attempts to show the development of this field and its revolutionary influence on the daily life of potential customers. The last chapter summarizes the previously discussed issues. It presents a model based on the concept of a strategy map, which shows relationships between the application of BI systems and potential enhancement of a company's value. The possible ways of connecting BI implementation with a company's business processes, conditions for the success of such projects, and potential threats and sources of failure are also discussed.

Finally, in the conclusion I reflect on the trends of BI development. The majority of the issues are illustrated with case studies of a hypothetical chain of ALFA stores. A chain store is a typical area of BI applications and gives a comprehensive picture of the subject. Each key issue is followed by a list of recommended reading and websites at the end of every chapter. I carefully selected every single recommendation so that readers could further explore the subjects of their interest. The recommendation list is of particular importance in the case of data-mining methods, where I purposefully refrain from mathematical formalism and make an attempt to support an intuitive understanding for the reader of the discussed methods. Still, I would like to encourage readers to familiarize themselves with the more formal attitude toward the analytical methods. All the examples of real BI tools that I give in this book are purely illustrative and as such should not be treated as recommendations of any kind.

This book is an introduction to the subject of BI and can potentially be used

- by students who study business administration,
- as supplementary reading for students in technical universities,
- by PhD and postgraduate students of economics and management,
- by researchers who specialize in business application of IT technologies.

It might also be useful for

- managers and members of the board of directors,
- consultants and business advisors,
- anyone who has a passion for practical applications of artificial intelligence methods.

Many thanks to my colleagues from the faculty of business administration in the Warsaw School of Economics for our discussions and their support, which contributed to the creation of this book. I also wish to express my gratitude toward the students who wrote their master's theses under my supervision for their assistance in designing the outline of a warehouse and demonstration reports for the case studies. I would like to particularly thank my wife, Ewa, and my son, Grześ, for the warmth that is always there regardless of the weather. Many thanks for your understanding when I annexed our kitchen table for a few months while engrossed in my work on this book.

Enjoy the book and feel free to send your comments to jerzy.surma @gmail.com.

Warsaw-Cambridge-Tyniec, summer 2010

CHAPTER 1

An Introduction to Business Intelligence

1.1. The Origins of Business Intelligence

During the 1970s Herbert Simon, a Nobel Prize winner in economics, was developing his world-famous concept of bounded rationality. He was certainly inspired by an interest in examining the cognitive boundaries of a man following the disappointing results of his own trials concerning the computer stimulation of human decision-making processes.[1] However, the intensive development of computer technologies gave him great hope for building systems to support human activities related to thinking and rational behavior. Those hopes were at least partly fulfilled thanks to the development of business intelligence (BI)—that is, a system that supports managerial decision making in enterprise management in the broadest sense of this word. A distinctive feature of BI is its powerful pragmatism: Out of the broad spectrum of technologies, only those that can be applied to business are selected. The four fundamental sources of information for BI and its tools are as follows:

1. *Statistics and econometrics*, including inter alia statistical theories of pattern recognition, econometric methods, statistical reasoning, and forecasting techniques
2. *Operations research*, including inter alia linear programming, decision theory, and game theory
3. *Artificial intelligence*, including inter alia heuristic search methods, machine learning, expert systems, genetic algorithms, artificial neural networks, and case-based reasoning systems

4. *Database technologies,* including inter alia data modeling, query languages, query optimization, and indexing methods

The application of computers in statistics and operations research resulted in the creation of so-called decision support systems. These systems required the application of formal mathematical models and were mainly based on quantitative data. Simultaneously, they naturally reduced the areas of use and application of computers in modeling real decision-making problems.

Artificial intelligence (AI) faced a much more challenging task. Work on AI was initiated in the 1950s, but to date it has not been crowned with any spectacular success. It was then a lesson in humility for the academic environment and proved how complex and refined human intelligence is. Nevertheless, thanks to those attempts numerous algorithms for supporting real decision-making processes were worked out that go far beyond the capabilities of decision support systems.

Although both AI and decision support systems had a large influence on BI, it was the development of database technologies initiated in the 1960s that was the most important. The development of databases based on the relational data model that allows for the relatively simple interpretation of business data and structured query language (SQL), which was easy to use for those times, proved to be particularly important. Progress in database technologies led to a boom in business applications of enterprise resource planning (ERP), which allows the standard processes of an enterprise to be automatic and well arranged. These transaction data (e.g., expense entering, invoice registering, and recording of bank account transactions or phone call records in a billing system) were soon discovered to be a source of interesting insights into the activities of a business. First, transaction data was aggregated into various reports, which were generated by decision support systems usually by means of SQL. Then techniques derived from decision support systems and artificial intelligence, which could conduct more sophisticated analyses, started to be applied. Those activities, performed at the turn of the 1970s and 1980s, were occasional and originally developed in two areas—namely, in shopping malls[2] and telecommunications companies.

1.2. BI as an Autonomous Discipline

In the 1980s, business applications became so advanced that a separate discipline of designing and creating databases for business decision support emerged. So-called data warehouses[3] and specialist toolsets appeared. Although the term "business intelligence" was first used in 1958 in a paper for *IBM Journal*,[4] a new sense was imparted to it by Howard Dresner from the Gartner company in 1988. Having analyzed the information technology (IT) market, he referred to business intelligence as to a kind of "umbrella" that covers numerous methods, technologies, and applications oriented to real business decision support in an enterprise:[5]

> *Business Intelligence* is a user-oriented process of gathering, exploring, interpreting and analyzing of data, which leads to the streamlining and rationalization of the decision-making process. Those systems support managers in business decision-making in order to create economy value growth of an enterprise.

Such a definition explicitly points out that BI is an IT management system and, strictly speaking, a third-generation IT management system.[6] In light of such an understanding of decision support systems, they encompass a broad spectrum of technologies, including the following:

- *Online analytical processing (OLAP) tools.* Software for multidimensional analysis of business data by integration, aggregation, and adequate mode of presentation and visualization of different data
- *Data-mining tools.* Algorithms for automatic analysis of great volumes of data using statistical and econometric methods, as well as machine learning methods that can analyze not only quantitative but also qualitative data
- *Knowledge management tools.* Tools that allow for storage, indexing, and analysis of textual documents and their further linkage with other data

This class of technological systems is based on the data collected by data warehouses—that is, database systems that gather data from various sources and make it readily available to businesses.

In the 1990s, BI became a widely known term among specialists, and on the level of tools, it was a standard offered not only by specialist companies but also by the greatest software manufacturers to enterprises, such as IBM, Microsoft, Oracle, or SAP.

1.3. BI and Company Management

At the beginning of the 21st century, IT technologies were developing extremely rapidly due to sudden Internet developments. Despite the almost total computerization of fundamental business processes, managers still have a fragmentary knowledge of their own businesses and often make decisions intuitively. Simultaneously, confusion caused by the excess of available data and a lack of its organization can be observed. Moreover, errors in data, lack of cohesion, and having a few versions of "the truth" in an enterprise have also led to a lack of trust in the gathered data. All of these factors aided the increased use of BI by enterprises. There are some sectors that already cannot do without such solutions—for instance, telecommunications and banking. The belief that analytical technologies are key tools to gaining a competitive advantage is also clearly visible.[7] Generally speaking, the successful development of BI contributed to the fulfillment of Herbert Simon's vision. According to his theories, the tasks managers deal with fall into three categories:[8]

1. *Supervising* the standard activities connected with the management of business processes and subordinates
2. *Solving well-structured tasks (problems),* that is, programmable decisions that are routine and repeatable and for which strict procedures have been worked out: For these tasks (e.g., establishing a selling price when logistics costs and purchase price are familiar), every single case does not have to be considered individually
3. *Solving ill-structured tasks (problems)*—that is, nonprogrammable decisions that don't have a cut-and-dried answer—related to new cases in which no pattern of behavior is established, results are

unknown, and there is also no ready-made solution (e.g., a strategic decision about starting up manufacturing abroad)

It should be stressed that at the moment BI is only applied to the first and the second category. The third category is definitely the most interesting one. At present, trials are being conducted in the application of BI methods as solutions for this type of problem. In order to understand the complexity of this issue, let us look at Table 1.1, which describes well- and ill-structured problems.

In formal terms, managerial tasks are decision processes, by which a decision means the selection of one possibility from a set of possible solutions. A BI system can generally support managerial decisions in the following ways (see Figure 1.1):

1. *Providing a decision maker with some information.* This mode encompasses the preparation of adequate information: business reports and outcome from complex analysis.
2. *Proposing managerial decisions.* This approach also includes the possibility of a system making decisions itself.[9]

Making decisions in supervision activities and solving well-structured problems can be supported by providing information and by proposing managerial solutions, while solving ill-structured problems might be supported by BI by their rationalization, that is, by providing the management board of an enterprise with suitable information (see chapter 3). However, proposing managerial solutions for ill-structured problems is not the subject of BI systems' activities.

Table 1.1. Well- and Ill-Structured Problems

	Well-structured problems	**Ill-structured problems**
Data	Quantitative, specific	Qualitative, unspecific
Knowledge	Mathematic model, algorithm	Experience, heuristics, intuition
Problem solving	• Procedure • Independence from context • Clearly specified, objective goals	• Ad hoc • Dependence from context • Vague, subjective goals

Source: Based on Turner (1988).

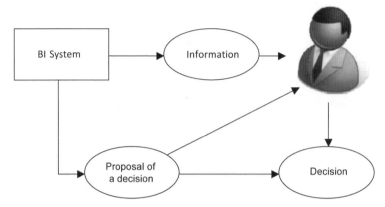

Figure 1.1. Support of managerial decisions by BI system.

Source: author.

1.4. Review of BI Applications in Some Business Areas

Applications of BI in four selected business areas are reviewed in Table 1.2. Each example is backed up by managerial information, which is

Table 1.2. Review of Some BI Applications

Area	Information	Insight	Decision
Customer management	Customer's lifetime value determined by the services provided to the customer	Analysis of the impact of the product portfolio and extra services on a customer's value	Reduction of additional services offered to the least valuable customers in order to reduce their service costs
Sales	History of sales expressed quantitatively and qualitatively according to product groups	Research into the impact of change in product price on the volume of sales	Correction of the prices of specific groups of products
Finance	Unit costs of product manufacturing connected to sales results	Analysis of profitability to specify the least profitable products	Modification of manufacturing process in order to reduce manufacturing costs
Logistics	Information on shipping routes connected to transport costs	Optimization of the routes to minimize transport costs	Modification of the procedure of route and transport selection

Source: author.

given to a decision maker, and solutions, which can be suggested on the basis of the information. Every decision is justified by analyses, which can be conducted in order to obtain certain recommendations.

Case Study 1.1 shows the use of BI concepts to fulfill a company's strategic initiatives. Subsequently, the second chapter of the book discusses the technological aspects connected with building BI systems.

Case Study 1.1

The chain store ALFA (a fictional store) is an important player in the market of discount stores with an ambition to become the leader in its business line. At present, its chain consists of several dozen stores spread across the northeastern United States. ALFA stores have identical exteriors, similar usable floor space, and an almost identical assortment of products: a few thousand indexes of groceries, cosmetics, tobacco, alcoholic beverages, newspapers, and so on. These stores are stocked from a logistics center (central warehouse) located in the center of the sales area (see Figure 1.2). The average customer is a middle-class person who prefers buying high-quality products or a great variety of products at a low price. The ALFA chain has a very effective procurement system, which has built a stable group of suppliers offering relatively low prices, and a selected assortment of ALFA's own brand of products. The chain competes against a few similar chain discount stores and shopping malls by offering low prices and an almost all-day availability of standard product offerings.

ALFA's management board is completely aware that because there is a limited diversification of products, it must focus on low prices and tight cost management to hold on to its competitive advantage. The fundamental strategic aim is to develop more quickly than its competitors (increase in the market share) and to improve its cost position. To realize its strategy, the board has formulated the following strategic initiatives (projects):

1. An intensive growth in market share by the rational selection of new locations and the fast opening of new stores in the chain

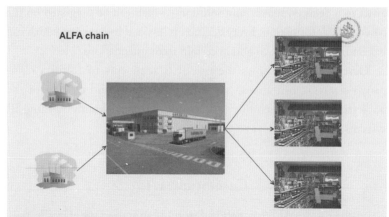

ALFA chain

Figure 1.2. The ALFA store chain network.

Source: author.

2. An increase in the average sales per store in comparison with competitors (benchmarking) by the selection of suitable product offerings, proper arrangement of products in the stores, and a quick response to changes in demand for individual products
3. Optimal cost management, mainly by a reduction of logistics costs

In taking steps to implement these strategic initiatives, the board was made aware that its management is based on intuition ("following one's nose") and that there is no suitable information about the chain store's performance, which results in an inability to manage it rationally. The following points were discovered:

1. The new store locations were selected in most cases intuitively without taking into consideration knowledge of how chain stores function in similar locations and available demographic data, environmental data, and so on.
2. The board and regional managers get the sales results from all the stores for individual products weekly. A weekly interval in the observation of sales of certain products makes it impossible to respond effectively to radical change in demand in comparison with projections.
3. The managers of the individual stores independently and intuitively arrange products on shelves and use floor space.

4. The divergence between the controlling department and the sales department was found by a calculation of logistics costs. Therefore, those departments give different results regarding the retail margin on a given product when logistics costs are taken into account (a problem of a few versions of the truth).

In order to deal with the aforementioned problems, a consulting company was hired. After preliminary research, it proved that the data registered in ALFA's IT system used are almost complete enough (after suitable processing and by means of some BI techniques) to provide information and support business decisions within the areas specified in Table 1.3.[10] After a suitable analysis of the requirements and an estimation of implementation costs, a strategic decision was made to implement a BI system.

Table 1.3. BI Requirement Analysis Table

Area	Provided information or analysis
Sales	• Quantity (volume) and amount of sales analysis divided into time period, sales region, product category, and so on. • Comparative analyses • Profitability analyses • Comparison with forecast sales • Rankings (e.g., top 25 or bottom 25 of products) • Research into seasonal character of trademarks • Analysis of impact of a price on sales
Logistics	• Analysis of product turnover in a logistics center • Inventory management by analyses of seasonal character of products • Availability of the product (i.e., if it is in stock)
Finance and controlling	• Margin analysis • Profitability analysis (ABC analyses using Pareto's principle)
Expansion (development of a chain store)	• Analysis of locations that connect the location of a store with its profitability
Merchandising	Market basket analysis: • Potential arrangement of products on shelves • Generating packages for promotions • Determining impulse products
Strategy management	• Managerial cockpit and indicators analyses • Comparison with business line (e.g., by making use of market data provided by benchmarking data)

Recommended Literature

Statistics

Aczel, A. (2005). *Complete business statistics* (6th ed.). New York, NY: McGraw-Hill.

Operations Research

Taha, A. H. (2010). *Operations research: An introduction* (9th ed.). New York, NY: Prentice Hall.

Artificial Intelligence

Nilsson, N. (1998). *Artificial intelligence: A new synthesis.* San Francisco, CA: Morgan Kaufmann.
Russel, J., & Norvig, P. (2002). *Artificial intelligence* (2nd ed.). Upper Saddle River, NJ: Prentice Hall.

Database Systems

Connolly, T. M., & Begg, C. E. (2004). *Database systems: A practical approach to design, implementation and management.* (4th ed.). Reading, MA: Addison Wesley.
Ullman, J. D., & Widom, J. (2007). *First course in database systems.* (3rd ed.). Upper Saddle River, NJ: Prentice Hall.

Business Intelligence and Decision Support Systems

Atre, S. (2003). *Business intelligence roadmap: The complete project lifecycle for decision support applications.* Reading, MA: Addison Wesley.
Turban, E., Sharda, R., & Dursun, D. (2010). *Decision support and business intelligence.* (9th ed.). Upper Saddle River, NJ: Prentice Hall.
Turban, E., Sharda, R., Dursun, D., & King, D. (2010). *Business intelligence: A managerial approach.* (2nd ed.). Upper Saddle River, NJ: Prentice Hall.

Case Study (Business Analytics for a Chain Store)

Westerman, P. (2000). *Data warehousing: Using the Wal-Mart model.* San Francisco, CA: Morgan Kaufmann.

Internet Resources

"Business Intelligence" on Wikipedia. http://en.wikipedia.org/wiki/Business
_intelligence
The Data Warehousing Institute. http://tdwi.org/
BeyeNETWORK. http://b-eye-network.com/

CHAPTER 2

The Data Warehouse

2.1. Introduction

In the first chapter, business intelligence (BI) was defined and a review of its possible applications in selected business areas was presented. The background for those solutions consists of basic BI tools. However, before we look at these in depth, we should look at the technological aspect of BI systems, that is, the structure of data warehouses. It seems obvious that the previous examples of business solutions use various data. However, this chapter answers the question of how data are collected and organized in order to be applied to business analysis.

Figure 2.1 shows the standard structure of a data warehouse. On the left, there are examples of sources of data—for example, logistics data in a transactional system. Within the sources of data, operational data are registered; this is data that is connected with isolated and specific business events. A possible use of a logistics system might be, for instance, to provide information that a given product is in stock. These data are sent to a data warehouse and adequately processed and connected with other data there. The information is read from the data warehouse (see the right part of Figure 2.1) to conduct certain business analyses. For example, information about the delivery and shipment of goods throughout a whole month might be used, within online analytical processing (OLAP), to detect those groups of products that fill the shelves. If these data are connected with information about the storage costs of different products, taken from a controlling system, then a complete analysis of the costs of storage of all goods that fill the shelves is possible.

It is essential to understand why data warehouses are built. There are at least four of them. Thanks to data warehouses you can

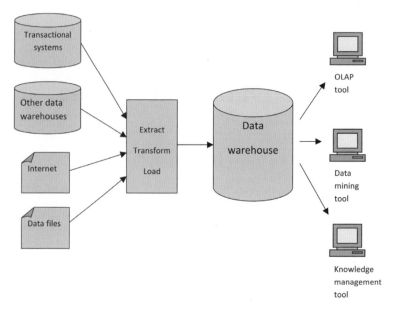

Figure 2.1. An example of the structure of a data warehouse.

Source: author.

- conduct business analyses without any interference in online transaction processing (OLTP).[1] Business analyses usually require complex and time-consuming calculations. However, this should not influence the daily operational work of systems that contain the source data. And thus, for instance, the sales analysis based on the aggregation of data from invoices registered in a transaction system ought not to cause delays in issuing invoices.
- obtain a global picture of a company's data—that is, you can integrate data from different sources, which gives a thorough picture of the business events in a given enterprise. For a telecommunications company, it could be information about the total sales value of a given client on the basis not only of the number of phone calls registered in the billing system but of the value of the accessories purchased by this client in brand stores (these data are registered in the sales system).
- gain access to historical data. Past information can be stored and then accessed later. Thanks to historical data, it is possible to carry out most basic business analyses.

- standardize information. The proper implementation of a data warehouse system enforces the standardization of terms and makes different departments of a company interpret performance indicators (measures) identically and calculate them in a homogenous manner. Consequently, the problem of many versions of the truth depending on the author of a given report is eliminated.

2.2. What a Data Warehouse Is

Bill Inmon is an American computer scientist and is recognized by many as the father of the data warehouse concept. His definition of a data warehouse is widely accepted.[2] A data warehouse is a subject-oriented, integrated, time-variant, nonvolatile collection of data in support of management's decisions.

"Subject oriented" means that the collected data are related to a specific business area—for example, a sales and marketing department. However, in practice, the data warehouse can include different business areas. The data warehouse is restricted to one business area or even to one department, usually called a data mart, which is a local warehouse that is generally a part of a corporate warehouse.

"Integrated" refers to the fact that all data are homogenous in their format, there is a range of acceptable values, and data are provided from most or all of an organization's operational system.

"Time variant" means that all data entered into a data warehouse have a timestamp, which allows companies to track changes and perform analytical research at certain time intervals.

"Nonvolatile" signifies that data, once entered into a warehouse, are remembered and cannot be deleted. After downloading, one can only read the data.

Technologically, data warehouses are operated through database management systems; usually these are databases using a relational model.[3] Inmon amended his classic definition of the data warehouse to include a corporate information factory (CIF).[4] This is a data warehouse that contains all the information resources of an enterprise and the data coming from the external world.

2.3. Logical Model: Star Schema

The way of modeling data in the data warehouse corresponds to the need for reporting of business data. When one makes a report, business measures are analyzed, such as sales quantity, in various contexts (i.e., dimensions), such as products, customers, and time. As Edgar F. Codd, a British computer scientist who invented the relational model for database management, observed, "in principle, there are a great number of different dimensions, which can be used to analyze a certain set of data. This complex perspective that is a multi-faceted, notional picture seems to be the way in which most business people perceive their enterprise."[5]

Table 2.1 shows a sales report of personal computers (PCs) by a computer hardware distribution company. In this report such measures as sales amount and costs for the product (e.g., purchase costs and logistics costs) are analyzed by looking at the dimension time (May 2008) and product (PC ABC, PC XYZ, and PC QWE).

In order to determine the data that are necessary to generate such a report, three tables must be defined:

1. A fact table (sales and costs; see Table 2.2)[6]
2. A dimension table (product; see Table 2.3)
3. A dimension table (date; see Table 2.4)[7]

A data warehouse model is able to link the separate data on sales, product, and date and then generate the report presented in Table 2.1. It should be pointed out that not all the data from the three tables were

Table 2.1. Demonstration of a Sales Report for a Computer Hardware Distributor, May 2008

Product	Sales amount ($US)	Costs ($US)	Profitability (%)
PC ABC	1,000,000	700,000	30
PC XYZ	2,000,000	1,800,000	10
PC QWE	2,000,000	1,500,000	25
Total	5,000,000	4,000,000	20

Note: Profitability (in %) = (qualitative sales – costs total) ÷ qualitative sales.

Source: author.

Table 2.2. A Demonstration Fact Table: Sales

ID_Product	ID_Date	Sales_Quantity	Price	Costs
P1	C5	500	2000	700,000
P2	C5	400	5000	1,800,000
P3	C5	1000	2000	1,500,000
P1	C6	400	2500	8,000,000

Source: author.

Table 2.3. A Demonstration Table for a Dimension: Product

ID_Product	Name	Producer	Processor
P1	PC ABC	Beta	Gamma
P2	PC XYZ	Delta	Gamma
P3	PC QWE	Beta	Theta

Source: author.

Table 2.4. A Demonstration Table for Dimension: Date (Time)

ID_Date	Month	Quarter	Year
C4	April	Q2	2008
C5	May	Q2	2008
C6	June	Q2	2008

Source: author.

used to generate the report and that the calculation of the sales amount requires reference to the sales table (Sales_Quantity and Price). Every line in every table has an unambiguous identifier: the primary key (PK).[8] In the product table, it is ID_Product; in the date table, it is ID_Date; and in the sales table, the pair ID_Product and ID_Date is the composite key. The sales table is connected with the product table by ID_Product. ID_Product in the sales table is then the so-called foreign key (FK).[9] The foreign key is a referential constraint between two tables. The foreign key identifies a column or a set of columns in one (referencing) table that refers to a set of columns in another (referenced) table. And analogically the sales table is connected with the date table by ID_Date; ID_Date is also a foreign key in the sales table. It is worth stressing that to one line (row) in the product table, zero, one, or many rows (records) in the sales table may correspond, while one row in the sales table may correspond exactly to one row in the product table. The sales table and the date table share exactly the same relationship. This type of relationship, described as *1:N* (one to many) is the basis of modeling data in a star schema (see Figure 2.2). Every rectangle corresponds to one table with data.

The schema presented in Figure 2.2 is called a multidimensional model, or popularly a star schema, because there are tables with dimensions connected by a relationship *1:N* in the fact table. In formal terms, the schema from Figure 2.2 should be described as follows:

- Sales (**ID_Product, ID_Date**, Sales_Quantity, Price, Cost)
- Product (**ID_Product**, Name, Producer, Processor)
- Date (**ID_Date**, Month, Quarter, Year)

Sales, product, and date are called entity sets. A single entity in a set presented in the table is simply a row in this table. Expressions in brackets are descriptions of attributes that are characteristic of a given set of entities. The bold selected attributes represent a key (an identifier) entity in the entity set. Owing to this convention, the schema in Figure 2.2 is called an entity relationship schema, and it is a classical way of modeling databases. In fact, having determined the format of data for specific attributes, one can already generate certain data structures in a selected database management system. The model in the form of a schema of entity sets is called a logical (conceptual) model, and its realization in a specific database is a physical model.

2.4. Sources of Data

Returning to the example of the report from Table 2.1, it is vital to understand how the fact table (i.e., Table 2.2) and other tables were filled

Figure 2.2. A demonstration dimensional model (star model).

Source: author.

in with data. For instance, in order to calculate the sales quantity for a given product, one must

1. check which transactional data system the source data (i.e., the invoices or orders, on the basis of which one can specify the quantity of sales) are stored in.
2. determine the interface between the system with the source data and the data warehouse and enter suitable data. Information from the given day should be added to the previous data to extend the history of sales by another day.
3. aggregate the data from the invoices, which are single transactional business events, to show the results for a whole month; take, for instance, the first row (Sales_Quantity in May 2008 for PC ABC) in Table 2.2. To calculate profitability, you must integrate sales data with the data related to costs, which are downloaded from a financial controlling system.

This simplified scenario shows the key issues connected with designing and using data warehouses. In general, there are the following sources of data:

- *Data files*. These could be both textual and electronic (e.g., Excel files).
- *Transactional systems*.[10] These are systems that, by making repeatable transactions, support the basic business processes of a company. The most popular among them are information management systems such as the following:
  ○ Enterprise resource planning (ERP), which supports companies in terms of finance, sales and logistics, warehouse management, production, procurement, human resource management, and so on
  ○ Banking systems for handling customers' accounts
  ○ Billing systems in telecommunications and energy companies
- *Internet data*. These could be both data taken from Internet pages and, for example, data mined by linking to Internet services that automatically transfer suitable information in the form of a subscription
- *Other data warehouses*.

It should be stressed that the sources of data may be located inside (and those are usually the most important) and also outside companies. The next chapter looks at where this information may come from.

Data from data sources are entered into a warehouse. This seemingly straightforward process usually consists of three phrases—extract-transform-load (ETL)—that are chronologically linked:

1. *Extraction* of data from sources of data. The identification of the sources of data is a complex issue, and you have to specify precisely the information that should be taken to obtain the suitable data (facts and dimensions). You have to refer to unambiguous business terms and connect them with specific data in the system. In some situations, it may turn out that not all the necessary data are registered. As a result, many times you are forced to prepare the source yourself, which is a very costly additional task.

2. *Transformation* of data to the form that allows for appropriate business application. This problem is related to, among other things, the integration of data:[11]

   • *Integration of formats*—that is, unification of formats of data coming from different systems. For instance, gender can be recorded in a number of different ways: m/f, M/F, male/female, and so on.

   • *Semantic integration*—that is, a uniform interpretation of data. The professional analysis of business requirements allows you to clarify, for instance, whether the sales are calculated on the basis of invoices or orders. If the sales are calculated on the basis of orders, it allows you to clarify whether this means orders received, carried out, and so on. If you are not precise at this stage and you do not work out an unambiguous definition of the term "sales," the problem of different versions of truth may arise. This applies also to tables with dimensions, particularly if a source system is not integrated and thus does not have standardized master data. Usually, the problem of uniform and unambiguous definitions for all terms used in warehouse is related to the issue of representation of metadata.

     Moreover, this also includes any additional activities, including, among others, the verification of the quality of the data and its preliminary aggregation before its input into the warehouse. The verification of the quality of the data consists of checking if a given date meets previously defined criteria (e.g., you can check whether personal details, including the date of birth of employees, fit in a rational range of values). The preliminary aggregation of data is, for instance, the input not of single transactions from the store's cash registers (i.e., receipts) but of summaries of the sales of each product for the whole day.

3. *Loading* of data into a warehouse. Normally, the loading of data into the warehouse is not a single action but a repeated process, in which data are added to the warehouse at strictly defined time intervals, depending on business needs: once per day, once per month, and so on. Consequently, the warehouse contains the history of business events that enables you to scrupulously analyze their changes over time.

This information demonstrates the importance of properly administering a data warehouse. To sum up, you should pay special attention to the significant difference between source data and data stored into a warehouse. The first type of data concerns operational processing in day-to-day activities in an enterprise, whereas the second one is related to management information, often at a strategic level, which enables you to gain insights into the company's performance from a number of angles.

2.5. Designing a Data Warehouse: Basic Facts

A data warehouse should be precisely designed to satisfy specific business needs. Usually, business requirements are specified by determining what information is necessary to manage a given business area. This allows you to select an appropriate logical model of a warehouse (see the star model) and then the necessary source data. This top-down approach was formulated by Ralph Kimball as a dimensional design model.[12] Kimball is widely recognized as one of the first architects of data warehouse logical models. According to this paradigm, there are four steps to design a data warehouse:

1. *Specify business requirements.* To understand business aims and needs in the context of existing source data, one must define the most important business issues in a given area. See, for instance, Table 2.1: It could be a decision to continue or discontinue selling a product on the basis of its profitability and how this changes over time.

2. *Declare the granularity.* Specify how detailed the data should be in the multidimensional model in the fact table. The most common is the lowest level of granularity, which is not subject to any further division. It definitely gives the greatest analytical flexibility, but it also may require more external memory than others. In the case of the previously mentioned computer hardware distributor, it would mean loading the data into the data warehouse for all the individual items from all invoices and all costs ascribed to the sale of a given product.

3. *Choose the dimensions.* Specifying the granularity determines the fact tables. In the presented example, it is the product dimension (defined as a concrete product; see Table 2.3) and the date dimension (defined as a concrete month; see Table 2.4).

4. *Identify the facts.* Specify precisely which business measures should be included in the fact table. Measures are quantitative, and various mathematical operations can be performed on them (e.g., the highest value, ordering, mean, sum). In the presented example, it is Sales_Quantity, Price, and Costs (see Table 2.2). The calculated measure—that is, Sales amount and Profitability (see the report in Table 2.1)—appears in the report generated for the user by a special tool for reporting as the result of a certain operation on the measures from the fact table.

The result of this four-step process of designing the multidimensional model is a star schema, such as the one in Figure 2.2. On the basis of this schema—that is, to be precise, on the basis of the definitions of sets of entities along with the specifications of data formats for attributes—you can easily create a proper data structure in database languages (e.g., structured query language, or SQL).

The example of modeling a data warehouse will be discussed in Case Study 2.1, and the basics of the business analysis will be presented in the next chapter.

Case Study 2.1.

The implementation of the BI system began with the analysis of business requirements. In the area of sales, it was as follows:

- *Area.* Sales.
- *Provided information or analysis:* Quantity (volume) and amount of sales analysis divided into time period, sales region, product category, and so on

According to guidelines on modeling a multidimensional model, the following activities were conducted:

1. Specify Business Requirements

To analyze business requirements, a sales report was produced providing the amount in percentage terms for selected product groups (in the example, four product groups) in a given period (in the example, January 2007) in stores in specific locations (in the example, stores in Boston). The sales report is shown in Table 2.5 and 2.6.

Table 2.5. Report: sales amount in January 2007

	Store name			
	ALFA_10	ALFA_11	ALFA_12	Total
Category	Sales amount	Sales amount	Sales amount	Sales amount
Juice	1470.05	1471.58	1820.68	4762.31
Dairy products	4432.69	4630.44	5073.86	14136.99
Confectionary	5981.00	6103.04	7558.79	19642.83
Cleaning products	929.52	1276.85	1259.43	3465.80
Total	12813.26	13481.91	15712.76	42007.93

Table 2.6. Report: sales amount (in percentage) in January 2007

	Store name			
	ALFA_10	ALFA_11	ALFA_12	Total
Category	Sales amount (%)	Sales amount (%)	Sales amount (%)	Sales amount (%)
Juice	3.50	3.50	4.33	11.34
Dairy products	10.55	11.02	12.08	33.65
Confectionary	14.24	14.53	17.99	46.76
Cleaning products	2.21	3.04	3.00	8.25
Total	30.50	32.09	37.40	100.00

2. Declare the Grain

The following level of granularity was defined:

- Date: 1 day
- Product: product item (SKU, or stock-keeping unit)
- Store: a single store

3. Choose the Dimensions

The following dimensions were defined:[13]

- Date (see Table 2.7)

Table 2.7. Dimension Date

Date
IDDate (PK)
Date
Full Date Description
Day of Week
Calendar Month
Calendar Quarter
Calendar Year

- Product (see Table 2.8)

Table 2.8. Dimension Product

Product
IDProduct (PK)
Product Name
SKU Number
Brand
Category
Package Type
Weight
Weight Units

In Table 2.9 are presented demonstration data for Product dimension.

Table 2.9. *Product: demonstration data*

Source: author.

IDProduct	Product name	SKU number	Brand	Category	Package type	Weight	Weight units
1	Chocolate bar Hit	1480	Chocolate bar	Confectionary	Elastic mat.	55	Grams
2	Yogurt Silk	3716	Yogurt	Dairy products	Elastic mat.	400	Grams
3	Buttermilk Joy	1600	Buttermilk	Dairy products	Elastic mat.	500	Grams
4	Chocolate Noir	3161	Chocolate	Confectionary	Paper	100	Grams
5	Crunchy-salty sticks	6008	Salty sticks	Confectionary	Foil	100	Grams
6	Crunchy-salty sticks	0855	Salty sticks	Confectionary	Foil	400	Grams
7	Washing Powder Shine	1025	Washing powder	Cleaning products	Foil	3	Kilos
8	Extra sweet & diet	2265	Beverage	Juice	Can	0,33	Liters
9	Milk chocolate bar	1973	Chocolate bar	Confectionary	Elastic mat.	45	Grams
10	Wafer Andrew	3008	Chocolate bar	Confectionary	Elastic mat.	40	Grams
11	Yogurt Super Cherry	1731	Yogurt	Dairy products	Elastic mat.	500	Grams
12	Kefir Agro	3530	Buttermilk	Dairy products	Elastic mat.	500	Grams
13	Qubus Small	0011	Beverage	Juice	Glass bottle	0,33	Liters
14	Qubus Big	0012	Beverage	Juice	Glass bottle	1	Liters

- Store (see Table 2.10)

Table 2.10. Dimension Store

Store
IDStore (PK)
Store Name
Store Number
Store Address
Store City
Store Manager
Store Region
Selling Square Footage
First Open Date

Table 2.11 presents demonstration data for Store dimension.

Table 2.11. Store: demonstration data

ID Store	Store name	Store number	Store address	Store city	Store manager	Store region	Selling square footage	First open date
1	Alfa_1	1489	Beacon St.	Newton	Jane Davis	MA	137	1-03-2004
2	Alfa_2	3711	Varsov St.	Newton	Trent Tucker	MA	174	1-07-2004
3	Alfa_3	1630	Morton St.	Newton	John Cash	MA	357	1-05-2004
4	Alfa_4	3216	Riverway	Bedford	Steve Lucky	MA	235	1-01-2004
5	Alfa_5	2600	John-Paul St.	Salem	Joe Turner	MA	256	1-09-2004
6	Alfa_6	1085	Tremont St.	Bedford	Horace Grant	MA	136	1-11-2004
7	Alfa_7	1102	Broadway	Burlington	John Novak	VT	185	1-03-2004
8	Alfa_8	2256	Wall St.	Burlington	Larry King	VT	214	1-10-2004
9	Alfa_9	1978	New St.	Newport	Jay Leno	VT	125	1-10-2004
10	Alfa_10	3080	Green St.	Boston	Scott Pippen	MA	115	1-11-2004
11	Alfa_11	1073	Main St.	Boston	John Paxson	MA	200	2-04-2005
12	Alfa_12	1353	Oxford St.	Boston	Michel Jordan	MA	203	1-04-2004

4. Identify the Facts

In Figure 2.3 the retail sales schema (multidimensional model) is presented where the fact table is: Transaction.

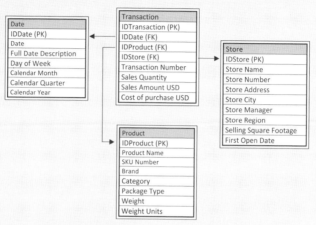

Figure 2.3. Retail sales schema (multidimensional model)

Source: Based on Kimball and Ross (2002)

In Figure 2.4 it is presented how to generate report (shown in Table 2.5) from the multidimensional model shown in Figure 2.3.

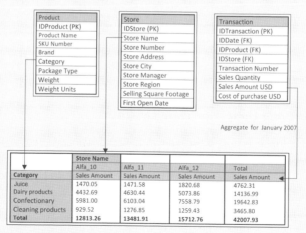

Figure 2.4. Dragging a dimensional attributes and facts into a simple report

Source: author.

In order to generate the required business reports, the following sources of data were specified:

- Cash registers, which register single transactions (receipts)
- ERP system, which includes master data (for dimensions)

Moreover, during the comprehensive analysis of business requirements, the following sources of data were defined:

- ERP system, which includes data about sales, purchases, and logistics costs
- Internet service that makes trade benchmarking data available
- Files
  - Planned sales (once a month)
  - Data concerning location (nearest competition, location, etc.)

Recommended Literature

Data Warehouse

Inmon, W. H. (2005). *Building the data warehouse* (4th ed.). New York, NY: Wiley.

Jarke, M., Lenzerini, M., Vassiliou, Y., & Vassiliadis, P. (2010). *Fundamentals of data warehouses* (2nd ed.). Berlin, Germany: Springer Verlag.

Database and Data Warehouse Design

Booch, G., Rumbaugh, J., & Jacobson, I. (2005). *Unified modeling language user guide* (2nd ed.). Reading, MA: Addison Wesley.

Imhoff, C., Galemm, N., & Geiger, J. (2003). *Mastering data warehouse design: Relational and dimensional techniques*. New York, NY: Wiley.

Kimball, R., & Ross, M. (2002). *The data warehouse toolkit: The complete guide to dimensional modeling* (2nd ed.). New York, NY: Wiley.

Silverston, L. (2001). *The data model resource book, Vol. 1: A library of universal data models for all enterprises*. New York, NY: Wiley.

Ullman, J. D., & Widom J. (2007). *First course in database systems* (3rd ed.). Upper Saddle River, NJ: Prentice-Hall.

Case Study (Dimensional Model for a Chain Store)

Kimball, R., & Ross, M. (2002). *Retail sales in the data warehouse toolkit: The complete guide to dimensional modeling* (2nd ed.). New York, NY: Wiley.

Internet Resources

The Data Warehousing Information Center. http://www.dwinfocenter.org/
Teradata University Network. http://www.teradatauniversitynetwork.com/
Ralph Kimball site. http://www.ralphkimball.com/

CHAPTER 3

The Basics of Business Analysis

3.1. Reporting and Data Analysis

3.1.1. Introduction

A data warehouse, which is created in accordance with your business requirements, allows you to analyze the data. If it is connected with suitable tools designed to analyze and present data, a systematic multidimensional data analysis can be made, which is called online analytical processing (OLAP).[1] As shown in Figure 2.1, the systematic analysis is directly linked to the end user.

According to Edgar F. Codd, "online analytical processing is multidimensional data analysis that is initiated by a business user and consists of complex reporting mechanisms, analyses and data visualization." Codd, who in 1970 formulated the relational data model, is considered to be one of the main developers and promoters of OLAP.[2] According to Codd, a systematic analysis tool should meet 12 conditions,[3] including application of a multidimensional model, an intuitive and flexible access to data, and also transparency: This is the isolation of the business user from the mode of data storage and connection with the source systems. In general, as Codd's conditions are purely technical by nature, they will not be discussed further.[4]

3.1.2. Online Analytical Processing

Online analytical processing consists of two fundamental elements:

- The multidimensional data model (discussed in chapter 2)[5]
- The operations set.[6] The tools that meet OLAP requirements are applied in two interconnecting areas:

○ *Provision of information.* The ability to devise reports in the desired order and in accordance with the required mode of data presentation; the ability to make queries ad hoc and allow for suitable distribution; the opportunity to spread information, automatic notification of events (alerts), and personalization of access.

○ *Analysis.* Analytical operations, which allow for the correct interpretation of the information provided and analysis of cause-and-effect relationships.

3.1.3. Data Model

Let us consider the example of a chain of used car dealers in Poland. Here the sales of used cars are analyzed in periods (Date) according to the brand of car (Product) and sales regions (Region). A corresponding multidimensional model is shown in Figure 3.1. The model in Figure 3.1 could be hard to interpret for a business user who is inexperienced in data modeling, and thus for OLAP the information is displayed as a multidimensional cube (see Figure 3.2).

In this model, cubes represent facts concerning sales (e.g., the measure is sales quantity) in the following dimensions: Region, Product, and Date. Usually, the multidimensional cube is an aggregate[7] of data registered on the level of the fact table, and its overall character is determined by all dimensions.

3.1.4. Basic Operations of Multidimensional Data Analysis

The basic operations of multidimensional data analysis are

Figure 3.1. The multidimensional model for a chain of used car dealers.

Source: author.

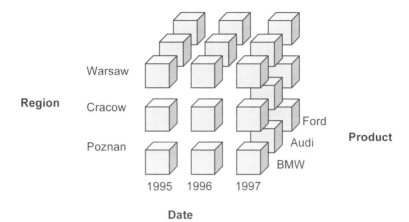

Figure 3.2. The multidimensional cube for sales in used car dealers.

Source: Wrembel, Bebel, and Zadrozna (2004).

- specification of the scope of analysis,
- drill down,
- roll up,
- slice and cube (selection),
- rotation,
- operations on measures.

3.1.4.1. Specification of the Scope of Analysis

The specification of the scope of analysis consists of determining what measures will be reported and in what dimensions they will be reported. Usually, the first operation specifies facts and dimensions for subsequent operations. Still, these settings can be modified during the analysis. For the cube from Figure 3.2, the Sales quantity and dimensions, Region, and Date in a correct report would look like the ones in Table 3.1 or in Table 3.2.

3.1.4.2. Drill Down

Drill down is one of the most common analytical operations that allows for the expansion of existing information. In the example in Figure 3.3, the sales analysis on the level of a calendar year is expanded to the level of a month in 1997. Such an effect can be achieved if a hierarchy is defined within the Date dimension,[8] for example, Year-Month-Day.

Table 3.1. Demonstration Sales Report for Used Car Dealers
(Version 1)

Date	Region	Sales quantity
1995	Warsaw	1,000
	Cracow	500
	Poznan	1,000
1996	Warsaw	1,500
	Cracow	500
	Poznan	900
1997	Warsaw	2,000
	Cracow	500
	Poznan	800

Source: author.

Table 3.2. Demonstration Sales Report for Used Car Dealers
(Version 2)

Sales quantity for			
	Region		
Date	Warsaw	Cracow	Poznan
1995	1,000	500	1,000
1996	1500	500	900
1997	2000	500	800

Source: author.

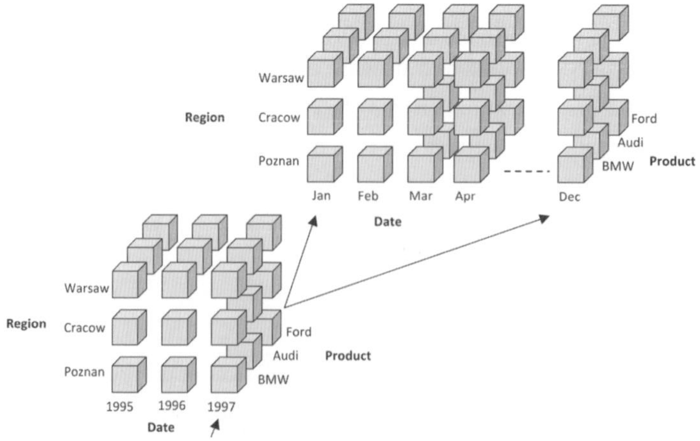

Figure 3.3. Drill-down in the dimension Date.

Source: Wrembel, Bebel, and Zadrozna (2004).

By drilling down this hierarchy, the sales analysis may be expanded to the level of 1 day. As long as it is semantically justified, you can formulate hierarchies within any dimension. For the Product dimension, it can be a car brand model. The lowest level in the hierarchy is connected with the level of granularity, which was discussed in chapter 2. For the cube in Figure 3.3, the report (for the measure Sales quantity and Region and Date dimensions) would look like the one in Table 3.3.

3.1.4.3. Roll Up

Roll up is the opposite operation of drill down, where for a given dimension, upward "navigation" in the hierarchy takes place to present more general aggregates.

3.1.4.4. Slice and Cube

In the slice-and-cube operation, facts are presented for a selected set of dimensions with specific values (either a concrete value or a set of values) for other dimensions. In Figure 3.4a, the Date dimension is sliced, while the cube in two other dimensions is limited to the year 1997. Analogically, in Figure 3.4b, the

Table 3.3. Demonstration Sales Report for Used Car Dealers After Drill Down in dimension Date

Sales quantity for			
	Region		
Date	Warsaw	Cracow	Poznan
01/1997	100	30	30
02/1997	120	20	20
03/1997	150	20	20
04/1997	200	30	30
05/1997	100	40	90
06/1997	190	50	100
07/1997	230	60	120
08/1997	200	70	100
09/1997	220	70	120
10/1997	220	30	60
11/1997	180	40	70
12/1997	90	40	40

Source: author.

slice of the Region dimension means that the presentation displays the sales values in all Dates and for all Products, but only for the Poznan region.

For the cube in Figure 3.4a, after the slice of the dimension "Date = 1997," the report (Sales quantity and Region, Product, and Date dimensions) would look like Table 3.4.

For the cube in Figure 3.4b after the slice in the "region = Poznan" dimension, the report (for the measure Sales quantity and Region, Product, and Date dimensions) would look like Table 3.5.

Table 3.4. Demonstration Sales Report for Used Car Dealers After the Slice in the dimension Date

Sales quantity for Date = 1997			
	Region		
Product	Warsaw	Cracow	Poznan
BMW	1000	150	300
Audi	500	250	300
Ford	500	100	200

Source: author.

Table 3.5. Demonstration Sales Report for Used Car Dealers After the Slice in the dimension Region

Sales quantity for Region = Poznan			
	Date		
Product	1995	1996	1997
BMW	200	300	300
Audi	300	300	300
Ford	500	300	200

Source: author.

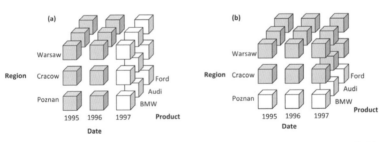

Figure 3.4. The operation of slice (a) dimension Date = 1997 and (b) dimension Region = Poznan.

Source: Wrembel, Bebel, and Zadrozna (2004).

3.1.4.5. Rotating

Rotating facilitates the presentation of data in the report. For the cube in Figure 3.5 (first phase), the start of the report (Sales quantity and Region and Date dimensions) would look like Table 3.6.

For the cube in Figure 3.5 (second phase), rotation by 90° vertically (with the Sales quantity and Region and Product dimensions) would look like Table 3.7. For the cube in Figure 3.5 (third phase) rotation by 90° horizontally (with the Sales quantity fact and Region and Product dimensions) would look like Table 3.8.

3.1.4.6. Operations on Measures

Operations on measures (numerical data) are a wide range of operations that are based on the numerical character of facts. The most common operations are as follows:

Table 3.6. Demonstration Sales Report for Used Car Dealers in the First Phase in the Operation of Rotating

Sales quantity			
	Region		
Date	Warsaw	Cracow	Poznan
1995	1,000	500	1,000
1996	1500	500	900
1997	2000	500	800

Source: author.

Table 3.7. Demonstration Sales Report for Used Car Dealers in the Second Phase in the Operation of Rotating

Sales quantity			
	Region		
Product	Warsaw	Cracow	Poznan
BMW	1,000	500	800
Audi	1,500	500	900
Ford	2,000	500	1000

Source: author.

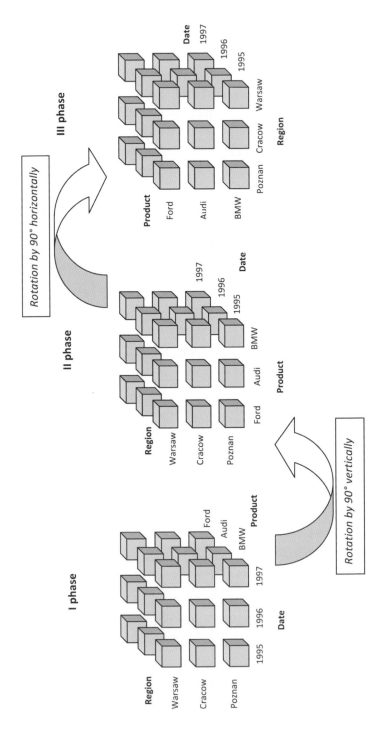

Figure 3.5. The rotation of the multidimensional cube.

Source: Wrembel, Bebel, and Zadrozna (2004).

Table 3.8. Demonstration Sales Report for Used Car Dealers in the Third Phase in the Operation of Rotating

Sales quantity			
	Product		
Region	BMW	Audi	Ford
Warsaw	1,000	1,500	2,000
Cracow	500	500	500
Poznan	800	900	1000

Source: author.

- Mathematical operations and functions, such as addition, the highest and the lowest value, the mean, and so on
- Ranking and sorting into groups
- Selection
- Calculation of new measures, for example (e.g., profitability; see Table 2.1)
- Basic statistical calculations

Case Study 3.1 shows a basic example of the OLAP analysis.

Case Study 3.1

To demonstrate operations, here is a further development of the previous case study (see Case Study 2):

- *Area:* Sales
- *Provided information or analysis:* Quantity (volume) and amount of sales analysis divided into time period, sales region, product category, and so on

The sales analyst was asked to check whether the expected (due to promotion activities) 20% growth in sales took place in May compared with April in stores located in Boston in the juices product category. During this period, the prices of juices were constant. Thanks to the newly implemented tool, the sales report (April compared with May) for the Category = "Juice"; Store City = "Boston"; and Calendar Year = "2007" was generated (see Table 3.9).

Table 3.9. Report: sales amount comparing April to May in 2007

Calendar month		
April	May	Grand total
Sales amount ($US)	Sales amount ($US)	Sales amount ($US)
954	1072	2026

The analyst saw that juice sales in May increased slightly, but the results were substantially lower than expected. He decided to carry on the analysis and, through drill down, see how the sales of each juice (Product Name) looked for the Category = "Juice"; Store City = "Boston"; and Calendar Year = "2007" (see Case Study 3.2).

Table 3.10. Report: sales amount in category Juice in April and May 2007

	Calendar Month		
	April	May	Grand Total
Product Name	Sales Amount USD	Sales Amount USD	Sales Amount USD
Qubus Big	295	230	525
Qubus Small	659	842	1501
Grand Total	954	1072	2026

To his amazement, he noticed that the sales of Qubus Big had dropped in May. In order to find the reason for this, the analyst limited the analysis exclusively to Qubus Big by selection and rotation. The sales of this product in April and May for different stores (Store Name) were as shown in Case Study 3.3 (Store City = "Boston"; Calendar Year = "2007").

Table 3.11. Report: sales amount in Boston stores in April and May 2007

	Calendar month		
	April	May	Grand total
Store Name	Sales amount ($US)	Sales amount ($US)	Sales amount ($US)
ALFA_10	98	128	226
ALFA_11	116	0	116
ALFA_12	81	102	183
Grand total	295	230	525

The report gave a surprising answer. It turned out that the sales of Qubus Big increased in two locations in Boston, while in the store ALFA_11, it amounted to zero (they didn't sell one single bottle of Qubus Big). Therefore, the low sales of juices in Boston resulted from a slump in sales of Qubus Big in ALFA_11. Finally, the analyst found the name of the manager (Store Manager) of this particular store in the report shown in Table 3.12.

Table 3.12. Report: Managers of stores in Boston

	Store city
	Boston
Store name	Store manager
ALFA_10	Scott Pippen
ALFA_11	John Paxson
ALFA_12	Michel Jordan

The analyst decided to show the result of his analysis to the regional sales director and suggested that he should contact John Paxson (the manager of the store ALFA_11). He also carried out a thorough analysis of sales and orders in the store ALFA_11 as compared with other stores in Boston.

3.2. Information Management

3.2.1. Introduction

The technological background of business intelligence (BI) has already been presented (the data warehouse, modes of presentation and data analysis by means of OLAP tools, etc.). Now the time has come to look at the business application of these technologies. Let us begin with an explanation of key terms, such as "data" and "information."

In his classic book about management, James Stoner[9] informally defined "data" as raw, unanalyzed numbers or facts—for instance, the volume of sales of the book *Witness to Hope* in May 2008. According to Stoner, information is organized and analyzed—for example, a sales analyst might compare the volume of sales of *Witness to Hope* in May and in April of 2008.

A formal definition of information is given by Bogdan Stefanowicz:[10] "Information describes meaning (content) which with suitable interpretation is given to a message M,"

$$\text{Message } M = < O, X, x, t >,$$

where O is a described object, X is an attribute of the object, x is a value of the attribute X, and t is time, in which the attribute X of the object O has the value x. In this definition, message M in the context of a specific semantic interpretation belongs to information, while as an object of processing and storage, it is data. It complies with the etymology of the word "information," which in Latin means "to shape" or "to give a form."[11]

All in all, technically speaking, data warehousing is about data storage and processing. However, in the context of a recipient (user), where data are provided by means of OLAP tools, you are likely to call it "information." According to the formal definition of information, the message <Book *Witness to Hope*, volume of sales, 44, 05/2008> is information about the fact that in May 2008, 44 copies of the book *Witness to Hope* were sold (although it is not information as understood in Stoner's informal definition). In fact, the result of the analysis of the sales trend—that is, the comparison between sales in May and April—is also information. You can have good insight into the relationship between data and information by looking at Figure 3.6, which also shows the final aim of information management, that is, supporting decisions.

As mentioned before, the subject (i.e., the recipient) of any information is always human. Given that fact and taking into account various possible functions of a person in an organization, you can single out two relevant kinds of information: managerial information and strategic information (see Table 3.9).

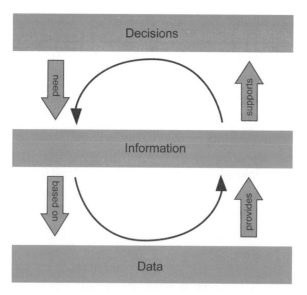

Figure 3.6. Relationship: data-information-decision.

Source: Reinschmidt, Gottschalk, Kim, and Zwieitering (1999).

Table 3.13. Type of Received Information Depending on Its Analysis and Recipient

Type of received information	Recipient	Analysis and supplementary information
Managerial	Heads, directors, board of directors	Detailed OLAP analyses, access to selected source data
Strategic	Board of directors, president, CEO	OLAP analysis, additional reports and explanatory analysis, study about competitors

Source: author.

This division complies with the development tendencies in BI, which are aimed at

- business processes management and realization (implementation) of a strategy (managerial information),
- strategic analysis and support for a planned strategy[12] (strategic information).

Illustrative of this is Table 3.14, which describes information at both levels:

- *Managerial information* tends to be provided mainly at the tactical and operational level of management but also at a strategic level.
- *Strategic information* is provided at a strategic level of management.

Table 3.14. Information in Managerial Decisions

Level of management	Period, time horizon	Frequency of update	Source	Credibility	Range	Level of granularity
Tactical and operational	Short, present	Big	Internal	Big	Narrow: inside the company	Big: analysis
Strategic	Long, future	Small	External	Small	Wide: environment, the world	Small: synthesis

Source: Based on Stoner, Freeman, and Gilbert (1995).

3.2.2. Managerial Information

3.2.2.1. Basics

Managerial information is information that is used in the management of a company.[13] In this chapter, this is limited to the analysis of the internal activities of an enterprise. To review the basic possibilities of providing decision makers with managerial information, Porter's value chain will be employed.[14] Michael E. Porter introduced the concept of the value chain as a tool to extensively explore the most important functions of an enterprise and the effectiveness of interactions that occur among them.

Porter's approach can be directly reflected in the process paradigm,[15] which defines an internal company process as follows: In a company, a process is a series of activities (tasks) designed to produce a product or a service.[16] According to the classic model, there are the following kinds of processes (see Figure 3.7):

- *Main processes.* They create and deliver products, services, or both offered on the market to external customers.
- *Supporting processes.* Products of these processes are invisible to external customers. They support main processes: resources or infrastructure management, among others.
- *Controlling (managerial) processes.* They ensure effective functioning of a company—for example, planning and budgeting, finance and strategic controlling, and monitoring the

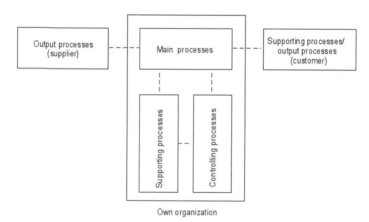

Figure 3.7. Typology of business processes.

Source: PROMET (1997).

realization of the strategy. Controlling processes are metaprocesses, as it were, because they support the management of other processes. For instance, controlling of production costs is used to streamline the production process and its management.

3.2.2.2. Review of Selected BI Applications

If you want to provide managerial information professionally, it will usually require creating a data warehouse, but in some applications it is possible to base your analysis on flat files with source data. Moreover, data processing can also be more complex than simple OLAP; it can be extended by various econometric models, operational research, or to be more general, by data-mining methods. Here only the basic applications will be presented—that is, applications of OLAP tools with some elements of basic statistical analyses. Applications that employ data-mining methods will be discussed in chapter 4.

Selected BI applications will be presented and divided into three process groups:

1. Main processes
   * Sales, marketing, and service (see Table 3.15)
   * Logistics (both internal and external; see Table 3.16)
   * Operations and production (see Table 3.16)
2. Supporting processes
   * Human resource management (see Table 3.17)
   * Supply chain management (see Table 3.17)
3. Controlling (managerial) processes
   * Finance (see Table 3.18)

BI systems in managerial processes should be of particular interest to readers of this book. Using source data from the integrated enterprise resource planning (ERP) systems, complex tools have been devised, which allow the following, among others things:

* Planning and budgeting
* Financial consolidation
* Stakeholder relationship management in terms of developing a suitable public relations policy in a company

Table 3.15. Review of Selected BI Applications (Managerial Information) on Main Processes in Sales, Marketing, and Service

Name	Description	Tool
Lifetime value analysis	Analytical model that describes the profitability of individual customers or groups of customers at specific time on the basis of the analysis of their activities (e.g., their shopping)	OLAP
Analysis of the deviation of sales of products of various assortments	Analysis of the influence of the amount of sold products, prices, and changes of assortment on the change of sales over time	OLAP
Price optimization (income management)	Analysis of the response of demand on the market to changes of prices, research into the impact of one's own and competitors' promotions, and the detection of optimal prices in certain distribution channels	OLAP with basic statistical functions (regression model for demand curve)
Analysis of sales profitability	Ratio analysis including the following: • Sales profitability indicator • Net profitability indicator • Cost indicator	OLAP

Source: Based on Davenport and Harris (2007).

Table 3.16. Review of Selected BI Applications (Managerial Information) on Main Processes in Logistics—Supply Chain Management and Production

Area	Name	Description	Tool
Logistics	Stocks analysis	The analysis of product rotation (seasonal character taken into account) to optimize warehouse management	OLAP with basic statistical functions
Logistics	Delivery analysis	Analysis of delivery in terms of its promptness and consistency with the order	OLAP
Production	Production effectiveness analysis	Analysis of productivity over time and in comparison with norms in terms of production line, machinery, shifts, and workers	OLAP
Production	Quality analysis	Analysis of the relationship between the quality of products and production lines or half-finished products depending on suppliers	OLAP with basic statistical functions

Source: author.

Table 3.17. Review of Selected BI Applications (Managerial Information) on the Supporting Processes in HR and Procurement

Area	Name	Description	Tool
HR	Training planning	Analysis of the profile of workers in comparison with formal requirements for a given position	OLAP
Procurement management	Ranking of suppliers	Ranking of suppliers depending on their promptness and the quality of supply	OLAP

Source: author.

Table 3.18. Review of Selected BI Applications (Managerial Information) on Controlling Processes in Finance

Name	Description	Tool
Analysis of financial reports (balance, profit and loss account, and cash flow account) and threat detection (early warning systems)	Evaluation of the financial situation and the results of the given enterprise by the analysis of its reports regarding the analysis of structure, dynamics, ratio analysis, cause analysis, regression and correlation analysis, and multidimensional comparison analyses	OLAP with basic statistical functions
Analysis of assets	Activity analyses based on inventory turnover, average collection period, and total assets turnover	OLAP
Costs analysis	Activity-based costing	OLAP with basic statistical functions
Profitability analysis	Identification of basic factors for sales profit and their influence on change of volume of sales, profitability ratios, gross profit margin, profit margin on sales, return on assets, return on equity	OLAP
Liquidity analysis	Liquidity analyses including the following: • Current ratio • Quick ratio • Cash ratio	OLAP
DuPont analysis	Measure of financial performance based on the two return on investment (ROI) equations: ROI (total assets) and ROI (equity).	OLAP

Source: Based on Schall and Haley (1991).

3.2.2.3. Business Processes Management

The use of BI systems to manage business processes in terms of monitoring and supervision is particularly important. It is based on the objective measurement of these processes by means of indicators (measures) of effectiveness called key performance indicators (KPIs). Standard critical success factors (CSFs) employed to assess the process, such as the completion date, cost, quality, and flexibility, imply a wide spectrum of KPIs, which are universally applied in practice by process specialists (see Figure 3.8).

In general, the performance indicator should have the following traits (according to the SMART[17] model):

- *Specific*. Is the measure clear and focused?
- *Measurable*. Can the measure be quantified and compared to other data?
- *Attainable*. Is the measure achievable, reasonable, and credible under expected conditions?

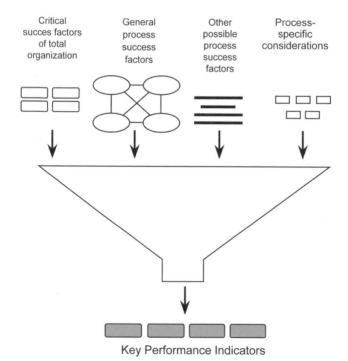

Key Performance Indicators

Figure 3.8. Generating KPIs based on CSFs.

Source: PROMET (1997).

- *Realistic*. Does the measure fit into the organization's constraints? Is it cost effective?
- *Timely*. Is the measurement doable within the given time frame?

Effectiveness indicators are implemented by BI systems in the form of a corporate performance management cockpit (management dashboard) and by means of data warehouses and OLAP tools (see Figure 3.9).

In this context, KPIs are described by the following parameters:

- Name of the process being monitored
- Name, definition, and formula describing the calculations
- Unit of measurement
- Frequency of update
- Measured period
- Specification of the forecast values, trends, or both at specific intervals
- Specification of the data sources
- Method of explanation for the value of the indicator by reports and operations (i.e., drill down)

Figure 3.9. Management dashboard (visualization of KPI and adequate OLAP reports) on the example of SAP Business Objects Strategy Management.

Source: SAP Poland (2009).

- Method of presentation for the end user
- Trade-off (i.e., impact of this indicator on other indicators)
- Connection with strategic goals
- Responsibility (responsible manager, which is usually the process manager)

The ergonomics of the visualization of indicators can even be reflected in the proper organization of the room used for board meetings (a possible solution is presented in Figure 3.10). To illustrate the issue of process management in which KPI monitoring is employed, let us consider order processing. This process is conventionally described by the on time in full (OTIF) indicator, which informs a logistics manager what percentage of orders are realized on time (promptness) and in full in a specific time frame (see Figure 3.11). In this example, OTIF is the KPI, which is directly subject to the processes of the manager's evaluation.

The maturity of BI solutions was one of the decisive factors in their development in business process management. BI can be employed for activities such as the following:

Figure 3.10. Management dashboard as an integral element of company's board meeting room.

Source: Daum (1999).

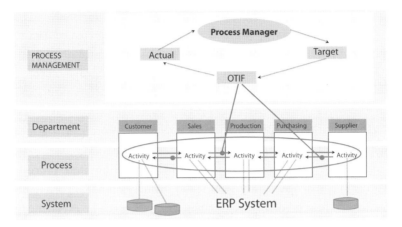

Figure 3.11. OTIF as an example of KPI in the order processing management.

Source: PROMET (1997).

- *Real-time monitoring.* Usually the time interval is not shorter than day, week, or month. Still, there are solutions that can be applied for real-time process monitoring. It is possible if the design of a data warehouse is directly integrated with the transactional system. In this approach, a specific transactional event is stored and aggregated almost immediately in the data warehouse. As a result, the information is pushed to the management dashboard.[18]
- *Analysis.* Every KPI as understood by multidimensional data analysis is a measure in the fact table or a calculated measure in the OLAP reporting tool. This means that all analyses discussed in this chapter are definitive for use.
- *Off-line simulations.* Cause-and-effect simulations and "if-then" analyses can be carried out, which enable a process manager to fully understand the process and search for suitable solutions in critical situations.
- *Suggestion of managerial decisions.* It is possible not only to provide managerial information but also to suggest business solutions on the basis of the current situation due to expert systems.[19] Despite being developed in the 1970s, this business application is not mature and universally applied yet.

- *Presentation and distribution of information.* It is universally used by corporate portals, in which the scope of presented data and mode of notification about critical or exceptional situations are defined, confidentiality of access is managed, mode of presentation is defined, and so on (see Figure 3.12).

Such applications of BI allow for comprehensive process management and its continuous improvement.

The development of the implementation of business processes within ERP management systems led to the development of referential models.[20] These models reflect the best practices based on experience of many enterprises that participated in the implementation of previous versions of the system. Consequently, it is now possible to construct ready-made models of data warehouses designed to provide concrete and business-oriented managerial information. Extensive ready-made referential data models (metadata repositories) are available for, among other things, concrete applications in telecommunications and the financial sector (e.g., banking).[21]

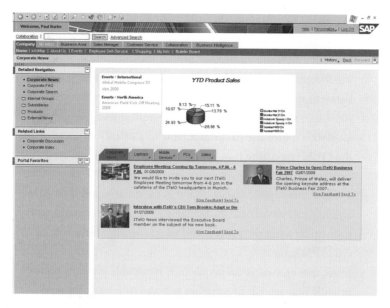

Figure 3.12. Example of personalized access to the corporate portal based on SAP Portal.

Source: SAP Poland (2009).

3.2.2.4. Balanced Scorecard

Research into the problem of strategy management and measuring a company's performance resulted in the concept of a balanced scorecard. This scorecard was drawn up by Robert Kaplan and Peter Norton as a response to the obvious weakness of the classical description of a company's performance by means of financial measures, in which intangible assets were gaining more and more importance.[22] Kaplan and Norton's concept showed its true worth when the scorecard was employed as a system of support for a company's strategy implementation and its rational management. This strategic scorecard is a tool that enables the management board to translate a company's vision and strategy into a set of logically linked KPIs in four perspectives: finance, customers, internal business processes, and learning and growth. The practical application of the balanced scorecard has spread thanks to the development of BI tools, which allow for the accurate calculation of the scorecard indicators at adequate time intervals and their visualization, description, and proper use in the management of a company. The values of all indicators are calculated and displayed for the same moment in time. Usually, this hinders cause-and-effect analysis because real connections between perspectives differ in time. Figure 3.13 shows a possible way to present a demonstration of KPI from selected perspectives.

A properly devised and implemented balanced scorecard is an extremely strong management tool. It can be employed, among others, to[23]

- present, clarify, and agree on the strategy inside the company;
- connect strategic aims with yearly budgets and indicators with forecast values;
- connect goals of different organizational units and different employees with the realization of the strategy;
- monitor strategic initiatives (projects);
- analyze the realization of a strategy systematically and periodically;
- gain feedback that allows for the updating and modification of a strategy;
- link the extent to which the strategic aims were achieved to the payroll system.

Case Study 3.2 shows an example of a management dashboard for a chain store.

Figure 3.13. Presentation of indicators of customer's perspective and perspective of the development of the balanced scorecard on the example of SAP Business Objects Strategy Management.

Source: SAP Poland (2009).

Case Study 3.2

Thanks to the implementation of the data warehouse and managerial information system, the management dashboard was devised for the president of the ALFA chain. This enables the president to monitor the enterprise's three key strategic initiatives: developing the chain, increasing the market share, and optimizing cost management. The ten KPIs on the management dashboard are shown below in Table 3.19:

Table 3.19. The ALFA chain KPI's

No.	KPI	Reporting period	Responsible
1	Earnings before interest and taxes (EBIT)	Month	Financial director
2	Return on capital employed (ROCE)	Quarter	Financial director
3	Cash conversion cycle (CCC)	Week	Financial director
4	Sales volume (amount & quantity)	Week	Board member responsible for sales
5	Market share	Month	Board member responsible for sales
6	Average store (Point of Sales) profitability	Month	Board member responsible for sales
7	Number of new stores	Month	Vice-president
8	Product turnover in the logistics center	Month	Logistics director
9	Logistics costs	Month	Logistics director
10	Staff turnover	Month	Human resources manager

3.2.3. Strategic Information

3.2.3.1. Introduction

In section 3.2.2, managerial information was intentionally limited to analysis of the internal activities of an enterprise (also in terms of the realization of the strategy; see section 3.2.2 on the balanced scorecard). However, here "strategic information" means information that supports the process of devising a strategy, which is mainly based on the analysis of the environment of the enterprise. The strategic analysis is then a series of activities designed to evaluate an enterprise and its environment, which allows for the creation of a strategic plan and its realization. On the whole, strategic management (including the analysis, planning, and realization of the strategy) is defined as making decisions that are supposed to take advantage of the opportunities and strengths of the company, avoid threats in the environment of the enterprise, and take notice of its weaknesses. Strategic managerial decisions, which are fundamental to the future of the company, are usually unique and by their very nature difficult to formalize. They concern activities that[24]

1. have long-term consequences,
2. build the competitive advantage of the company,
3. effectively exploit the company's main reserves and capacity,
4. are internally consistent.

And that's why they are usually

1. ill-structured,
2. performed in times of great uncertainty,
3. costly (because they require clear-cut and often irreversible investment decisions),
4. cascading (i.e., to be effective, they must be followed by a series of consistent tactical and operational decisions).

According to Herbert Simon's works,[25] this kind of decision is labeled as an ill-structured task. Solutions for this task are found using strategic information supported by the use of strategic analysis. A relatively long-term perspective and dependence on external sources of information are particularly important here (see Table 3.14).

Strategic analysis, including demand for information, encompasses three areas:[26]

1. *Enterprise itself.* This area is connected with managerial information (see section 3.2.2).
2. *Competitive environment.* This includes external individuals, groups, and companies with which the enterprise has business relations: suppliers, customers, competitors, and so on.
3. *Macroenvironment.* This includes political, technological, legal, demographic, and social conditions.

The competitive and macro environments are connected to the issue of "competition intelligence." In American specialist literature, this approach to the theory and practice of enterprise environment analysis was originally called "competitor intelligence."[27] However, its semantic range has been extended over time. Nowadays, competitive intelligence (CI) is defined as the activity of monitoring an enterprise's economic and competitive environment, which is relevant for strategic decision making.[28] This terminological digression is extremely important because the term "business intelligence" is mistakenly interpreted as competition intelligence. Although BI and CI are very different in many ways, they do partially overlap. From the point of view of BI, CI is the field (subset) of applications in the context of supporting strategic managerial decisions. From the point of view of CI, BI may be interpreted as a set of tools and technologies for more effectively drawing up and processing strategic information.

3.2.3.2. The Process of Strategic Information Management

The process of strategic information management (see Figure 3.14) is carried out by a panel of experts called information brokers. The recipients of this strategic information are the board of the company.

The process of strategic information management consists of the following stages:[29]

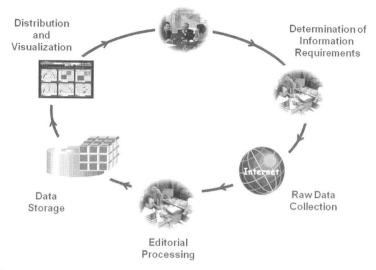

Figure 3.14. The process of strategic information management.

Source: Fulleborn and Meier (1999).

1. *Determination of information requirements.* This analysis is made with the board of the company and aims to determine the key intelligence topics and key intelligence questions designed to support (rationalize) strategic decisions.

2. *Raw data collection.* Having determined the information requirements, the sources of information are located and the raw data are collected. As mentioned before, these are usually external sources of unstructured data: They may amount to 95% of all sources, of which the vast majority are published and public sources. Unpublished data, which are collected during interviews with employees, experts, and so on, is also taken into account. When online databases or Internet sources are the source of data, additional opportunities arise connected with making queries, which allow for searching web pages, their constant monitoring, and often the identification of previously unknown sources of information.

3. *Editorial processing and data storage.* This is the key stage of the whole process, which consists of processing the collected raw source data and transforming it into strategic information. The issue of selectiveness plays a vital role at this stage. As was observed by Herbert Simon,[30] the problem does not lie in the scarcity of information but in its proper

selection so that decision makers can have access to the most important information.[31] The key factors here are the broker's very clear understanding of the enterprise board's needs, which should have been determined at the first stage; the wider market context; the ability to select adequate information, and finally their synthesis. It must be stressed that current information technology (IT) allows for only limited support of these activities. Then this stage naturally leads to the storage of data in the data warehouse, which allows for its further processing, analysis, visualization, and distribution.

4. *Distribution and visualization of information.* The final stage is the drawing up of the managerial information and its distribution to the board. The key is the ability to select the essential information and present it clearly. Having more sources of information at their disposal than the rest of the employees, leaders can sometimes lose their sense of direction more easily or follow the wrong track. Extensive knowledge and the proper synthesis of information enable managers to detect implicit relationships and anomalies, and most importantly, they make them more sensitive to things that are strategically vital.

3.2.3.3. The Role of BI in Strategic Information Management

BI systems designed to support strategic decision making are often called strategic information systems. These BI systems start the process by collecting the source information. This collecting takes place on the web, and extract-transform-load (ETL) techniques (see section 2.4) can be employed to integrate various sources of data for further analytical processing.

The most demanding part of the process is connecting sources of information in which the stored data are largely unstructured. The crucial point is to connect text documents with quantitative data—for instance, the financial results of the company with its product strategy report. Technically, it is possible to store data of different types in a data warehouse, but only if they are connected with each other through the primary key or identifier (see Figure 3.15).

If quantitative data describing companies, competing businesses, or both are properly stored, benchmarking can be conducted on the level of key performance indicators. At present, competitive benchmarking is one of the standard management techniques and consists of comparing

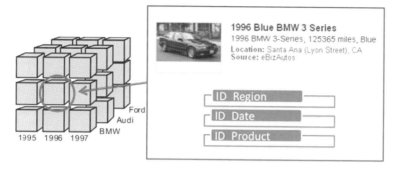

Figure 3.15. Example of connecting text data in the data warehouse.

Source: Based on Fulleborn and Meier (1999).

competing enterprises and their activities. Making comparisons with a company's competitors on the level of KPI is relatively easy. The difficulty lies in the fact that data from external sources are nonnumerical (qualitative) and usually unstructured (i.e., they are in various formats or lack clear-cut and consistent nomenclature, uniqueness, etc.). The classic methods of data processing (see chapter 2) are of no use in such a situation. And that means that most of the work at this stage is performed manually by a team of information brokers. However, at least part of the processing can be initially done by automatic text data processing by means of text mining.[32]

Text data exploration consists of mining data from unstructured text data. The following methods can be employed for text mining:

- *Text categorization.* Automatic matching of the document with formerly determined categories (e.g., putting dot-com documents about competitors into one of three categories: new products and technologies, current events, or other).
- *Text clustering.* Automatic identification of sets (groups) of documents that are similar because of one shared feature (e.g., the most frequent identical key word). For each identified group, statistics are quoted (e.g., the most important shared features of each group). In this approach, it is possible to identify duplicate and almost identical documents.
- *Data extraction.* Extracting from a text document some objects that have shared semantic interpretation, such as people, organizations, places, things, events, and also relationships between

identified objects (see Figure 3.16). Here it is also possible to identify the language of the text or interpret abbreviations used, dates, units of measurement, and so on.

- *Editorial processing.* Automatic processing of a document in terms of spellchecking (i.e., correcting spelling and punctuation mistakes) and summarizing (i.e., identifying the most important tasks and putting them together into a consistent text).

The last stage—that is, the visualization and distribution of information if the data are stored in the data warehouse—is processed in the same way as the previously discussed management dashboards. The fundamental difference lies in the necessity of presenting text data.

Our examination of the basics of business analysis concludes with a reflection on the importance of strategic information. In the next chapter, advanced business data analysis methods will be presented.

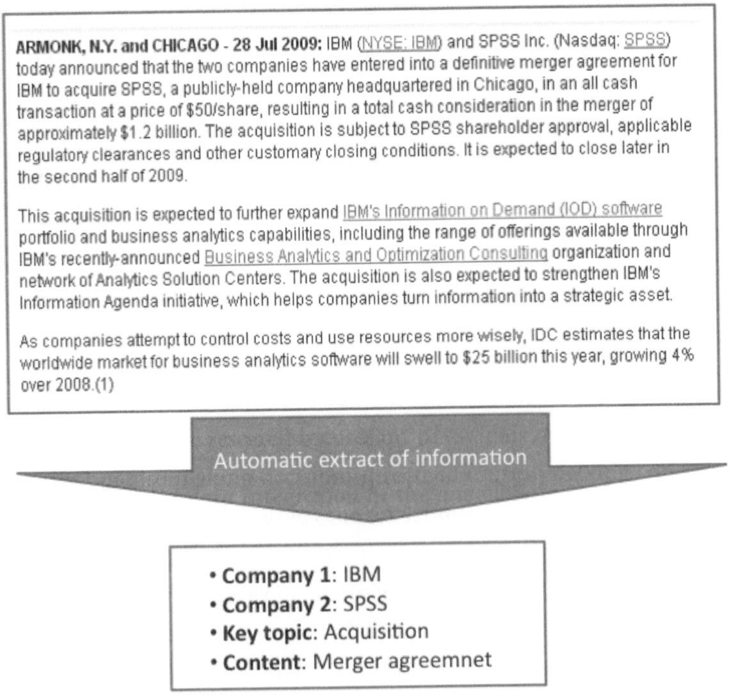

ARMONK, N.Y. and CHICAGO - 28 Jul 2009: IBM (NYSE: IBM) and SPSS Inc. (Nasdaq: SPSS) today announced that the two companies have entered into a definitive merger agreement for IBM to acquire SPSS, a publicly-held company headquartered in Chicago, in an all cash transaction at a price of $50/share, resulting in a total cash consideration in the merger of approximately $1.2 billion. The acquisition is subject to SPSS shareholder approval, applicable regulatory clearances and other customary closing conditions. It is expected to close later in the second half of 2009.

This acquisition is expected to further expand IBM's Information on Demand (IOD) software portfolio and business analytics capabilities, including the range of offerings available through IBM's recently-announced Business Analytics and Optimization Consulting organization and network of Analytics Solution Centers. The acquisition is also expected to strengthen IBM's Information Agenda initiative, which helps companies turn information into a strategic asset.

As companies attempt to control costs and use resources more wisely, IDC estimates that the worldwide market for business analytics software will swell to $25 billion this year, growing 4% over 2008.(1)

Automatic extract of information

- **Company 1**: IBM
- **Company 2**: SPSS
- **Key topic**: Acquisition
- **Content**: Merger agreemnet

Figure 3.16. Example of automatic extraction of information from the text.

Source: author.

Recommended Literature

Business Analytics and Managerial Information

Davenport, T. H., & Harris, J. G. (2007). *Competing on analytics.* Boston, MA: Harvard Business School Press.

Davenport, T. H., Harris, J. G., & Morison, R. (2010). *Analytics at work: Smarter decisions, better results.* Boston, MA: Harvard Business School Press.

Kaplan, R. S., & Norton, D. P. (1996). *The balanced scorecard: Translating strategy into action.* Boston, MA: Harvard Business School Press.

Williams, S., & Williams, N. (2007). *The profit impact of business intelligence.* San Francisco, CA: Morgan Kaufmann.

Competitive Intelligence and Strategic Information

Day, G. S., & Schoemaker, P. J. (2006). *Peripheral vision: Detecting the weak signals that will make or break your company.* Boston, MA: Harvard Business School Press.

Rainer, M. (2008). *Competitive intelligence: Competitive advantage through analysis of competition, markets and technologies.* Berlin, Germany: Springer Verlag.

Web Mining

Linoff, G., & Berry, M. (2002). *Mining the web: Transforming customer data into customer value.* New York, NY: Wiley.

Markov, Z., & Larose, D. (2007). *Data mining the web: Uncovering patterns in web content, structure, and usage.* New York, NY: Wiley-Interscience.

Text Mining

Feldman, R., & Sanger, J. (2006). *Text mining handbook: Advanced approaches in analyzing unstructured data.* Cambridge, UK: Cambridge University Press.

Weiss, S., Indurkhya, N., Zhang, T., & Damerau, F. (2004). *Text mining: Predictive methods for analyzing unstructured information.* Berlin, Germany: Springer Verlag.

Internet Resources

OLAP

Data Warehousing and OLAP. http://www.daniel-lemire.com/OLAP

OLAP Report. http://www.olapreport.com/

Information Management

Business Intelligence Journal. http://www.businessintel.org/
Business Process Management Initiative. http://www.bpmi.org/
Balanced Scorecard Institute. http://www.balancedscorecard.org/

Strategic Information

Strategic and Competitive Intelligence Professionals. http://www.scip.org/
The CI resource Index. http://www.bidigital.com/ci
Open Source Intelligence. http://www.onstrat.com/osint/
EUROSINT Forum. http://www.eurosint.eu/

CHAPTER 4

Advanced Business Analysis

4.1. Introduction

The main aim of the approaches previously discussed was to provide decision makers with suitable information. It is possible to identify this information if you precisely define the monitored key performance indicator (KPI) or if an analyst formulates adequate queries during the analysis. They usually ask and then answer the questions "What happened?" (reporting), "Why did it happen?" (analyzing), and "What is happening now?" (monitoring). But the most intriguing are the questions about the future: "What will happen?" (extrapolation and prediction). Additionally, we can often discover unexpected connections (regularities) in the given business area. This can be achieved thanks to data-mining methods, which stem from techniques derived from statistics and algorithms of machine learning.[1] Data mining is defined as "the nontrivial extraction of implicit, previously unknown, and potentially useful information (patterns) from data."[2]

Data mining is often called knowledge discovery in databases. The most vital element of this knowledge discovery is the identification of patterns, which are then defined against the background of the structure. The structure is a global summary of the database. The pattern in this context describes the structure, which refers to a relatively small part of the data, that is, reduced (local) space.[3]

Usually, the result of data-mining algorithms is understood as knowledge (see Figure 4.1) of which we were not previously aware. Knowledge, according to its definition in an encyclopedia, is all credible information about reality and the ability to use it. Sticking precisely to this definition, and particularly to its second part, the result of data mining cannot be treated as knowledge. However, as the term is popularly understood, such an interpretation seems to be

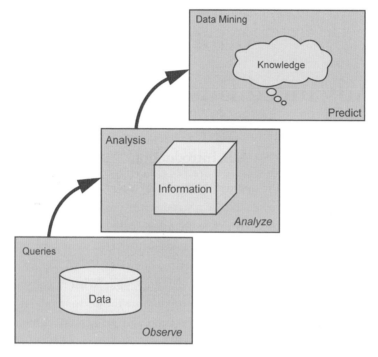

Figure 4.1. Data mining: from data to knowledge.

Source: Reinschmidt, Gottschalk, Kim, and Zwieitering (1999).

acceptable because classic data analysis consists of answering a given question through data analysis. Advanced analysis enables you to go even further, which allows you to discover things that were not formerly known because there was no reason to ask about them. Therefore, you find out something new about a given area of reality and this can be regarded as discovering knowledge.

The most common applications of data mining in business are classification, prediction, cluster analysis, and mining association rules:[4]

1. *Classification* is assigning an object to a predefined category. Usually decision trees, neural nets, or k nearest neighbors, for instance, are used.
2. *Prediction (or estimation)* is similar to classification, but it assumes that the category to which you assign the object has a continuous set of values. Such prediction is usually used for forecasting, for which you often use regression decision trees, artificial neural nets, and standard statistical methods.

3. *Cluster analysis (or clustering)* consists of finding in the set of objects subsets (groups) of objects that have similar features (i.e., are highly homogenous). It is often called "taxonomy," "cluster analysis," or popularly in marketing "segmentation post hoc."

4. *Mining association rules* involve searching sets (usually pairs) of objects that appear together in a given context. These objects are linked to each other (by association), which means that the presence of one object implies with a certain probability the presence of the object that is linked to it.

Later on, classification, cluster analysis, and association principle discovery will be discussed separately from prediction and estimation, which is commonly known from statistics.[5]

4.2. Classification

In business, decision trees are commonly used for classification.[6] Their big advantage from a user's point of view is that they provide an explicit and clear representation of knowledge. The central idea of decision trees, as understood by John Ross Quinlan,[7] and the algorithm used by decision trees will be discussed by looking at an example of a basic system that supports credit decisions (loan applications) in a retail bank.[8]

The decision to grant credit is an example of classification that consists of putting a credit application described by a set of descriptive attributes into one of two categories: to grant the credit (YES) or to deny it (NO). To conduct classification, you have to define a classifier, which would enable you to categorize objects (i.e., credit applications) into one of at least two previously defined categories (classes; see Figure 4.2). A borrower is described by four descriptive attributes and one decision attribute that describes the decision made in the credit process (see Table 4.1). A demonstration classifier has the form of the decision tree (see Figure 4.3). As seen in Figure 4.3, in the internal nodes of the decision tree, there are selected attributes; branches represent values of a given attribute, while leaf nodes (terminal nodes) stand for the classification decision. Therefore, this tree represents the following knowledge about classification of credit applications expressed in the formula "if . . . then . . .":

Table 4.1. The Description of Attributes for Classification of the Credit Application

Kind of attribute	Attribute	Set of values
Descriptive	Risk group	{low, medium, high}
Descriptive	Education	{primary, secondary, high}
Descriptive	Income forecast	{optimistic, pessimistic}
Descriptive	Guarantee	{full, partial, no}
Decision	To grant a credit	{YES, NO}

Source: author.

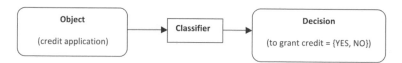

Figure 4.2. Classification of new objects.

Source: author.

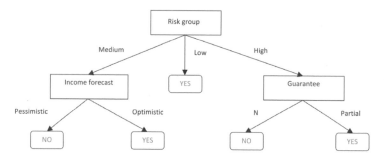

Figure 4.3. Classifier: Decision tree for the classification of a credit application.

Source: author.

- *If* Risk Group = medium and Income Forecast = pessimistic, *then* Grant a Credit = NO
- *If* Risk Group = medium and Income Forecast = optimistic, *then* Grant a Credit = YES
- *If* Risk Group = low, *then* Grant a Credit = YES
- *If* Risk Group = high and Guarantee = no, *then* Grant a Credit = NO
- *If* Risk Group = high and Guarantee = partial, *then* Grant a Credit = YES

Usually, this set of rules is supplemented by a default rule, which applies if none of the classifier rules is met by a categorized object. Let us now consider how you construct a classifier. The fundamental idea consists of learning (generating a decision tree) on the basis of learning examples (learning set; see Figure 4.4). Learning examples are examples of correctly categorized (classified) objects. For our example in Table 4.2, 14 examples from the history of credits granted by a bank are shown. Each example has a concrete value for four attributes that describe a credit application and a clear-cut classification decision (see the definition of attributes in Table 4.1). For every example, "YES" means that the credit was properly repaid, and "NO" signifies that there were some setbacks (including, among others, lack of repayment) and the borrower should not have been given credit approval.

In the described example, the learning system from Figure 4.4 will be represented by algorithm ID3.[9] It is one of the most common algorithms for building decision trees based on top-down induction. It works as follows:

1. Name A the best attribute (according to the information gain test) for the next node (during the first iteration, it is a root) of the tree.
2. For each value of A attribute, create a branch with the next node of the tree.
3. Divide each set of teaching examples into subsets for each value of the Attribute A.
4. If all examples have the same decision, create a leaf node and stop. If not, then start again (from step 1) for each of the newly created nodes.

The key step of algorithm ID3 is the first step, which consists of specifying an attribute that will appear in the node of the tree. Intuitively,

Figure 4.4. Learning the classifier from learning examples.

Source: author.

Table 4.2. Learning Examples to Build a Classifier for Credit Applications

Example	Risk group	Education	Income forecast	Guarantee	To grant credit
P1	medium	high	pessimistic	partial	NO
P2	medium	high	pessimistic	no	NO
P3	low	high	pessimistic	partial	YES
P4	high	secondary	pessimistic	partial	YES
P5	high	primary	optimistic	partial	YES
P6	high	primary	optimistic	no	NO
P7	low	primary	optimistic	no	YES
P8	medium	secondary	pessimistic	partial	NO
P9	medium	primary	optimistic	partial	YES
P10	high	secondary	optimistic	partial	YES
P11	medium	secondary	optimistic	no	YES
P12	low	secondary	pessimistic	partial	YES
P13	low	high	optimistic	partial	YES
P14	high	secondary	pessimistic	no	NO

Source: author.

you should choose an attribute whose values will divide a set of examples into maximum homogenous subsets in the context of being assigned to decision classes.

Figure 4.5 shows how the third step of algorithm ID3 would divide all learning examples into subsets for each of descriptive attribute. As you can see, the attribute "Risk Group" seems to divide the best elements of the set of examples into homogenous sets, and for the value "low," the set is almost entirely homogenous and has the value "YES" for the decision attribute. In algorithm ID3, information gain serves as an attribute selection method:

$$\text{Gain } (S,A) = \text{Entropy } (S) - \text{Entropy } (S|A),$$

where Gain (S,A) is the expected reduction in entropy caused by knowing the value of attribute A, Entropy (S) is the entropy connected with the classification of the set of examples S, and Entropy $(S|A)$ is the entropy of the division of the set of examples S according to the attribute A.

The lower the value of Entropy $(S|A)$, the greater the organization (purity)—that is, the homogeneity of the classification for examples

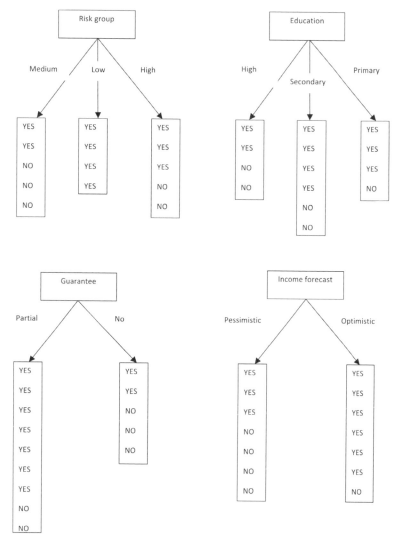

Figure 4.5. Division of set of examples according to selected attribute.

divided into subsets. For our example, suitable information gain has the highest value for the attribute "Risk Group":[10]

- Gain (S, Risk group) = 0.246 bit
- Gain (S, Education) = 0.029 bit
- Gain (S, Income forecast) = 0.151 bit
- Gain (S, Guarantee) = 0.048 bit

Therefore, this attribute should appear first in the root of the tree (see Figure 4.3). You should also notice that the algorithm did not use all information included in the set of learning examples. The attribute "Education" turned out to be of no use while generating the tree, and as a result, it has no influence on the decision made about granting credit.

This classifier in the form of the decision tree for making credit authorizations is obviously purely illustrative. In reality, the whole process of constructing a credible classifier—including, for instance, choice of attributes, preparation of a set of learning examples, parameterization of the chosen algorithm, and finally its testing—is a challenging task that demands considerable work and experience.[11]

4.2.1. Limitations

To construct a classifier on the basis of a set of examples, you need to solve many problems that are common for the majority of data-mining algorithms. However, if you are aware of these limitations, you should have reasonable expectations regarding their possible applications and the quality of the knowledge generated by them. This awareness also gives methodological guidelines concerning learning and testing techniques. The main problems are connected with induction, history, updating, and overfitting.

4.2.1.1. Induction Problem

Learning from examples is inductive reasoning. You make credible generalizations on the basis of a limited set of observations. This is the fundamental limitation of inductive conclusions: You are unable to prove that a given inductive conclusion is true. However, you can falsify it unambiguously.[12] Inductive reasoning maintains falsity, which means that if facts that are subject to generalizations are not true, inductive conclusions are also not true, but true facts do not necessarily bring you to true conclusions. Therefore, by definition you should treat every inductive conclusion as uncertain.

4.2.1.2. History and Updating

The process of generating a classifier involves learning on the basis of historical observations. It seems to be obvious that the fragment of reality described by this classifier is subject to changes in time. This is a key issue, particularly in business applications, in which the classifier may have become outdated even a relatively short time after the learning process (e.g., as a result of rapid changes in the market). This is then another fundamental factor that influences the uncertainty of classification. In fact, the classifier needs to be updated on the basis of new observations, whereas the more obsolete examples should be forgotten. There are some techniques to construct an incremental decision tree that take into account new learning examples without the necessity of building a whole new tree from zero.

4.2.1.3. Overfitting

A standard verification of classifiers is based on the examples from the testing set. The classic phenomenon that results from too deep learning based on learning set it is called overfitting. A tree into which too many classifications fit and that reflects the learning examples perfectly is usually highly complex and has very little ability to generalize. An illustration of this is the graph in Figure 4.6. The X-axis represents the complexity of the tree reflected in the number of nodes, while the Y-axis represents the accuracy of the classification calculated by the quotient of accurately fitted examples (numerator) and the number of all examples (denominator). The continuous graph represents classification accuracy on trees that have learned and been tested on the same series of examples (learning set). As you can see, it is an increasing function that almost reaches 1. It is more important to analyze the graph that is marked with a dotted line; the tree is based here on the set of learning examples (learning set) and tested on a separate set of test examples (test set). When the tree is a certain size (approximately 20 nodes), more complex trees are more closely adjusted to the learning set (see the continuous graph) and generalization is more and more difficult (see the dotted line). According to Tom Mitchel,[13] overfitting is a problem not only of decision trees but also of other algorithms in machine learning. Here this problem is resolved by reducing the size

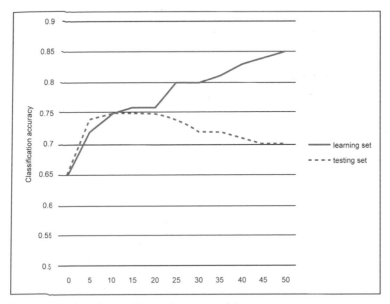

Figure 4.6. Overfitting during learning of decision trees.

Source: Based on Mitchell (1997).

of the tree by pruning: You remove some less-important fragments (sub-trees) from the complete decision tree.

Case Study 4.1 shows the interpretation of outcomes generated by using the decision tree approach.

Case Study 4.1

One of the main strategic initiatives achieved by the implementation of the strategy was a rapid growth in the market share of the company. This was realized by improving the selection procedures for locations of new stores and rapidly opening new stores in the chain.

As this initiative was being carried out, it was observed that the new locations of stores in most cases were selected intuitively without recourse to information about the functioning of other chain stores in similar locations and without access to demographic and business data. The effects of business intelligence (BI) implementation to date, technological tools (the data warehouse), and the desire to take advantage of information technology (IT) assets convinced the board of directors to continue using advanced analytical methods to support the decision-making process in the choice of new locations.

Previously, the decision about opening a new store and its location was made by the member of the board responsible for chain development on the basis of a specialist's recommendation. This recommendation was based on

1. confirmation of the required legal and formal status for a new store,
2. a location report including factual and photo documentation and the situational plan describing the business environment of the store,
3. the specialist's intuitive evaluation based on his long-standing experience.

The board of directors decided to experimentally apply data-mining methods to find out whether they could use them to support the traditional procedures for selection of new locations. This was a classification task that included the following considerations:

- Descriptive attributes included information about the location of the store, such as total floor space, number of citizens within a 1000-meter radius, number of passersby, competitors within a 500-meter radius, number of parking places, description of the business environment, description of location, and so on. Geomarketing data purchased from an external company were also taken into account, including information about saturation of the target group around the store and suitable demographic and socioeconomic data.
- The decision about the desired profitability of the store was made and divided into three types:
  - *League 1.* Profitability considerably above the desired level of profitability
  - *League 2.* Profitability within certain limits (target values)
  - *League 3.* Profitability close to the desired level of profitability or below it

After looking at the aforementioned data, stores were classified based on the following type of rules:

If certain location, *then* store of certain type =
{1 league, 2 league, 3 league}.

Thanks to such a set of rules, the board of directors was able to predict how the store would potentially operate in a given location. The board of directors decided to construct a classifier in the form of a decision tree. To create a learning and test set, information about the locations and profitability of stores in cities with a population above 50,000 and with a similar demographic and economic profile was used. Consequently, a 300-element set of examples was constructed, which for better differentiation consisted of a comparable number of stores from only leagues 1 and 3. Of this set, 200 elements (learning sets) were used to generate the classification rules. The generated tree was tested on the remaining 100 elements of the set and included 50 examples from league 1 and exactly the same number from league 3 (test set). The results are:

Test examples (set)	Classified as league 1	Classified as league 3
Fifty examples from league 1	40	10
Fifty examples from league 3	20	30

The classification accuracy[14] was to 0.7. This result proved to be satisfactory. However, the problem of incorrect classifications was brought to light. The classifier classified 20 examples from league 3 as league 1, and 10 league 1 stores were classified as league 3. Such a situation carries with it substantial business costs both if the company opts for YES for an unsuitable location or if the company opts for NO for a suitable location, which would result in lost sales. In the context of this analysis of the initial results, the board of directors decided to continue working to improve the quality of the classifier before it is applied to support real decisions about locations.

4.3. Cluster Analysis

Cluster analysis consists of finding in a set of objects subsets (groups) that have common attributes (features). The cluster analysis algorithm aims to divide a set of objects into subsets in which interclass similarity is maximized and intraclass similarity is minimized. Whereas in a classification task you have to classify objects, in clustering your task is to find classes into which objects can be divided. That is why learning classification principles are called *supervised learning* and the identification of groups of objects is called *unsupervised learning*.

The key issue in cluster analysis is finding similarity between objects. If objects are described by quantitative attributes (sales amount, financial liquidity, etc.), you usually employ similarity measures based on the notion of distance and the Euclidean measure for calculations. It is more difficult to calculate similarity if the attributes are qualitative (e.g., attributes in Table 4.1). In such situations, you use techniques to transform qualitative attributes into quantitative ones so that you can finally use measures based on the notion of the distance between objects in space whose dimensions are described by attributes.[15]

One of the most popular approaches to cluster analysis is the *k*-means algorithm.[16] It works as follows:

1. Choose *k* observations by random (number *k* is given a priori) as one-element classes, which will serve as the cluster center (center of gravity).
2. Assign each observation to the nearest class (the most similar cluster center).
3. Calculate the new cluster center for every *k* class.
4. If the cluster center has not changed significantly, you should stop here. If not, go back to step 2.

In Figure 4.7, the *k*-means algorithm is shown in the space of two attributes, where *k* = 2. The circled points represent the cluster center. In practice, the algorithm finishes when, for all groups, objects assigned to them remain in them without changing their membership.

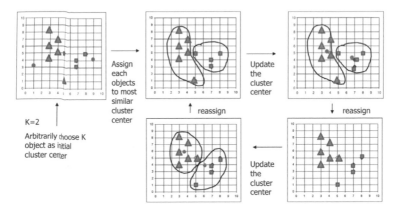

Figure 4.7. Example of k-means algorithm.

Source: Yang (2008).

Clustering is commonly used in marketing research. In the classic approach, market segments are given a priori in an arbitrary manner. Consequently, their further analysis depends on the accuracy of this choice. In the case of the cluster analysis algorithm, the segments are automatically discovered by the algorithm and reflect real connections between customer groups, which are often based on latent (implicit) attributes—this is called *post hoc segmentation*.[17] A review of selected business applications of cluster analysis methods is shown later, in Tables 4.5 and 4.7.

4.4. Association Rules

Mining association rules consist of searching groups of objects that appear together in certain contexts. This task is performed by means of association rules analysis.[18] Market basket analysis, in which you want to find out which products are most frequently sold together in one basket, is as a classic example.[19] Let us consider a simple example of association rules analysis by looking at the following example of four market baskets. Each line in Table 4.3 represents a market basket registered on the receipts in a cash register.[20] You can use these receipts to analyze the frequency of certain pairs of products. In Table 4.4, the frequency of the simultaneous presence of two products for all possible pairs is shown. Table 4.4 gives the following information about sales:

Table 4.3. Example of a Set of Receipts

Receipt	Product names
1	Juice, water
2	Milk, juice, bread
3	Juice, beer
4	Juice, beer, water

Source: author.

Table 4.4. Frequency of the Simultaneous Presence of Pairs of Products in the Market Basket

	Juice	Bread	Milk	Water	Beer
Juice	4	1	1	2	2
Bread	1	1	1	0	0
Milk	1	1	1	0	0
Water	2	0	0	2	1
Beer	2	0	0	1	2

Source: author.

- Sales of juice are very good because this product appears in every single basket.
- Juice is relatively often sold together with water and beer.
- Milk is never sold together with beer or water.

Such conclusions would be well grounded if the sample of the market basket had an adequately high statistical significance. The essence of mining association rules during market basket research lies in formulating principles such as "if one puts product A into a basket, then it is highly plausible that he or she will put product B into a basket as well." The accuracy of such a principle in the context of a conviction that such an event took place is described by two parameters: support and confidence:[21]

- *Support* describes how often products A and B appear together in the basket against all transactions.
- *Confidence* describes the conditional probability of putting product B into the basket if product A has been put there earlier.

Let us, for instance, consider the following rule: "*If* there is juice in a basket, *then* water is also in a basket." For this principle with shopping, as in Table 4.3,

- support = (number of baskets with juice and water) ÷ (number of all baskets) = 2 ÷ 4 (50%),
- confidence = (number of baskets with juice and water) ÷ (number of all baskets with juice) = 2 ÷ 4 (50%).

Let us also consider the opposite principle to understand things more clearly: "*If* there is water in a basket, *then* juice is also in a basket." Notice that support for this rule will be exactly the same, but confidence will be higher:

- confidence = (number of baskets with juice and water) ÷ (number of all baskets with water) = 2 ÷ 2 (100%).

This means that (for a given sample of baskets) putting water into a basket always implies the purchase of juice.[22] Figure 4.8 shows all possible combinations of rules and their parameters: support and confidence.

	If	Then	Support (%)	Confidence (%)
1	beer	juice	50.000	100.000
2	juice	beer	50.000	50.000
3	beer	juice, water	25.000	50.000
4	water	juice, beer	25.000	50.000
5	water, beer	juice	25.000	100.000
6	juice	water, beer	25.000	25.000
7	juice, beer	water	25.000	50.000
8	juice, water	beer	25.000	50.000
9	bread	juice	25.000	100.000
10	juice	bread	25.000	25.000
11	bread	juice, milk	25.000	100.000
12	milk	juice, bread	25.000	100.000
13	milk, bread	juice	25.000	100.000
14	juice	milk, bread	25.000	25.000
15	juice, bread	milk	25.000	100.000
16	juice, milk	bread	25.000	100.000
17	milk	juice	25.000	100.000
18	juice	milk	25.000	25.000
19	**water**	**juice**	**50.000**	**100.000**
20	**juice**	**water**	**50.000**	**50.000**
21	beer	water	25.000	50.00
22	water	beer	25.000	50.00
23	bread	milk	25.000	100.000
24	milk	bread	25.000	100.000

Figure 4.8. Example of association principles.

Source: author.

Association rules can be presented graphically, as shown in Figure 4.9. Each product is represented by a circle, and its size corresponds to the frequency of the presence of a given product in the baskets. The vector between the two circles represents the association rule, and its thickness is connected with the parameters of the evaluation of the rule.

Knowledge about connections between sales of products can be used for

- arrangement of products on store shelves,
- promotional packages,
- recommendation of upselling,
- comparative research of stores and taking into account the factor of time in carrying out research (mining sequence patterns).[23]

Obviously, these applications go beyond the environment of chain stores and can be useful in other business areas.[24] It is particularly worth stressing that they can support upselling: You can analyze a customer basket in time and consequently suggest rational solutions.

4.4.1. Limitations

There are two vital limitations of both cluster analysis and association rules analysis that are of great importance for other data-mining methods as well: the problems of interpretation and computational complexity.

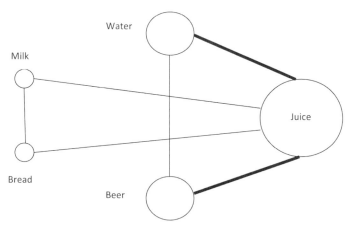

Figure 4.9. Example of graphical representation of association rules.

4.4.1.1. The Problem of Interpretation

In general, rules derived from association rules algorithms only slightly contribute to knowledge that was not previously known and would simultaneously be useful for business purposes. In most cases, those rules are trivial and do not go beyond our current knowledge. There is also a separate group of rules in which interpretation is problematic in business areas. These rules are therefore usually omitted because of their incidental and unclear character. Similarly, the interpretation of classification rules is also dubious. Another problem is business interpretation of segments generated automatically by cluster analysis algorithms. The proper identification (interpretation) of important segments and the rejection of those that are not useful in business require the analyst to have a profound knowledge of the market. In fact, it is a problem that concerns other data-mining algorithms and is a real limitation to its business applications.

4.4.1.2. The Problem of Computational Complexity

You can easily imagine how much data must be processed by the algorithm based on receipts from a chain of stores. There are millions of records even in a relatively short time period. The number of product indexes in an average chain usually reaches a few thousand. The issue becomes even more complicated if you take into account not pairs of products but three or more product items. The complexity of the analysis increases sharply, which carries with it unacceptable times of generating the rules.[25] This problem applies to most algorithms for discovering knowledge and is one of the basic limitations of these approaches.

4.5. Other Methods

The aforementioned techniques are only a selection of the most popular ones in business applications. There is a wide spectrum of other approaches that derive mainly from statistics. An extremely interesting group of techniques are those inspired by the computer simulation of natural phenomena. The human brain has been an inspiration for a long time, and within works on artificial intelligence, numerous computer simulations of neural networks[26] have been carried out. Although this work has so far been unsuccessful in simulating human thinking, it has been tremendously effective in solving classification and prediction tasks. Another technique derived from man's observations of nature is the genetic algorithm, which is based on research into theories of evolution and genetics.[27] This approach worked out a lot of concrete solutions, which are in most cases applied to resolving optimization problems. However, this is rarely used in business. One of the key elements in proving the reliability of data-mining analyses is the possibility of explaining (clarifying) suggested answers (e.g., by showing a path of reasoning in a decision tree to justify credit decisions). Both artificial neural networks and genetic algorithms do not justify explicitly the solutions they generate and are a sort of black box in the process of supporting decisions.

4.6. Review of Selected BI Applications in Terms of Data Mining

The following is a review of selected BI applications of data-mining methods for main and controlling processes:

1. Main processes
   - Sales, marketing, and service (see Table 4.5)
   - Internal and external logistics (see Table 4.6)
   - Operations and production (see Table 4.6)
2. Controlling processes
   - Finance (see Table 4.7)

Case Study 4.2 shows the results of a pilot study using a market basket analysis. The subsequent chapter shows how BI systems can be used to analyze human behavior.

Table 4.5. Review of Selected BI Applications (Advanced Analysis) in Sales, Marketing, and Service

Name	Description	Tools
Analytical customer relationship management (CRM)	Data analysis system based on the registration of events concerning a relationship with a customer, that is, analysis of customer preferences and behavior in order to generate accurate decisions about upselling, suggesting suitable promotions, and buying new products. Can be achieved by accurate segmentation of the market and the calculation of customer live time value.	OLAP, data mining (classification, clustering, association rules), statistics (forecasting methods)
Churn vs. retention	Analysis of reasons for recent customer abandonments and finding plausibility of current customers' ones. Commonly used by, for example, telecommunications operators in order to devise suitable marketing campaigns or improve relationship with customers who are likely to abandon.	OLAP, data mining (classification and clustering)
Conjoint analysis	Analysis of customer preferences in the context of the influence of different product qualities (quality, price, functionality, service, etc.) on a decision to buy a given product.	Econometrics (analysis of variance)
Chi-square automatic interaction detection (CHAID) analysis	Segmentation of customers according to influence of certain descriptors (age, education, gender, etc.) on possibility of repeat choice of the product of the same brand.	Econometrics (automatic interaction detection model)
Recency, frequency, monetary (RFM) analysis	Segmentation of customers based on customer behavior in the context of recency (time from recent purchase), frequency (number of purchased products over certain time), and monetary value (value of purchased products over certain time). On the basis of such, an analysis of upselling and cross-selling strategies are devised.	OLAP, data mining (clustering)
Response model	Forecasting who in a given group of customers will respond to an offer on the basis of analysis of history of behavior of a similar group of customers. Used to in marketing campaign management.	Econometrics (regression analysis, prediction), data mining (classification)

Source: author.

Table 4.6. Review of Selected BI Applications in Logistics and Production

Area	Name	Description	Tools
Logistics	Demand planning	Using historic sales data for forecasting. It is often used by chain of stores because it enables you to discover which products are seasonal (etc.) and as a result to manage supply chain effectively.	Data mining (regression trees), statistics (forecasting methods)
Logistics	Optimization of trade routes	Mapping out of optimal route according to which you can reach in a certain order destination with minimal costs.	Operational research (transportation problem)
Production	Operations management	Supporting decisions concerning amount of resources you should allocate to certain activities ordered to perform a given task.	Operational research (techniques for solving resource allocation problems)

Source: author.

Table 4.7. Review of Selected BI Applications (Advanced Analysis) in Finance

Name	Description	Tools
Bankruptcy prediction	Use of financial analysis of an enterprise to construct early warning systems in the context of possible bankruptcy.	Data mining (classification algorithm, for instance discrimination function analysis)
Fraud detection	Used, for example, in banking; it is the analysis of different frauds in financial transactions to find patterns of criminal activities. By monitoring of current transactions and use of such patterns, you can locate current fraud attempts.	OLAP, data mining (classification and clustering)
Risk modeling	Analysis of financial risk in services and products where payment is postponed. A classic example is the analysis of credit ratings.	OLAP, data mining (classification and clustering)

Source: author.

Case Study 4.2

Within the scope of strategic initiatives, ALFA's board of directors concluded that it was extremely important to improve the chain's sales volume. One of the recommended methods for improving sales was to optimize the arrangement of products on the shelves to increase sales. To perform this task, the board decided to employ a market basket analysis and, after generating the association rules, modify the arrangement of products in its stores.

To verify the validity of this approach before applying it in the whole chain, a pilot study was carried out. The sample was 50 stores in which all receipts from a whole month were registered. The algorithm was parameterized in such a way (adequate values for support and confidence) that it generated rules only for pairs of products. The study resulted in a set of rules, which were divided into three groups:

1. *Trivial rules* (approx. 60%). Self-evident knowledge, usually previously known and used
2. *Incomprehensible rules* (approx. 30%). Knowledge that is difficult to interpret, not justified in business, or of no use in practice
3. *Useful rules* (approx. 10%). Vital and previously unknown knowledge that can be directly used for new arrangement of products

On the basis of the useful rules, modifications were introduced in some stores (in which the volume of sales was being monitored) and compared with test stores (in which products were not rearranged). Apart from the new arrangement of goods, salespeople were given special instructions on how, on the basis of the customer market basket, to convince customers to take advantage of upselling of products located near the checkout. After 3 months, the result of this comparison study convinced the board to make a systematic market basket analysis for all its stores and then implement the results across the whole chain.

Recommended Literature

Introduction to Data Mining

Han, J., & Kamber, M. (2006). *Data mining: Concepts and techniques* (2nd ed.). San Francisco, CA: Morgan Kaufmann.

Nisbet, R., Elder, J., & Miner, G. (2009). *Handbook of statistical analysis and data mining applications.* Amsterdam, Netherlands: Academic Press.

Classification

Breiman, L., Friedman, J., Olshen, R., & Stone, C. (1984). *Classification and regression trees.* Belmont, CA: Wadsworth International.

Duda, R. O., Hart, P. E., & Stork, D. G. (2000). *Pattern classification.* New York, NY: Wiley-Interscience.

Quinlan, J. (1993). *C4.5: Programs for machine learning.* San Francisco, CA: Morgan Kaufmann.

Cluster Analysis

Anderberg, M. (1973). *Cluster analysis for applications.* Amsterdam, Netherlands: Academic Press.

Association Rules

Adamo, J. (2000). *Data mining for association rules and sequential patterns: Sequential and parallel algorithms.* Berlin, Germany: Springer Verlag.

Neural Nets

Hertz, J. A., Krogh, A. S., & Palmer, R. G. (1991). *Introduction to the theory of neural computation.* Reading, MA: Addison-Wesley.

Genetic Algorithms

Michalewicz, Z. (1996). *Genetic algorithms + data structure = evolution programs.* Berlin, Germany: Springer Verlag.

Data Mining in Business Applications

Berry, M. J., & Linoff, G. S. (1999). *Mastering data mining: The art and science of customer relationship management.* New York, NY: Wiley.

Berry, M. J., & Linoff, G. S. (2004). *Data mining techniques: For marketing, sales, and customer relationship management.* Indianapolis, IN: Wiley.

Rud, O. (2000). *Data mining cookbook: Modeling data for marketing, risk and customer relationship management.* New York, NY: Wiley.

Case Study (Market Basket Analysis for a Chain Store)

Corinne, B. (2001). *Mining your own business in retail using DB2 intelligent miner or data.* IBM Form No. SG24-6271-00. IBM Redbooks.

Internet Resources

KD Nuggets. http://www.kdnuggets.com/

Data Mining Group. http://www.dmg.org/

Index of Machine Learning Courses. http://www.cs.iastate.edu/~honavar/Courses/cs673/machine-learning-courses.html

Tom Mitchell Machine Learning textbook. http://www.cs.cmu.edu/~tom/mlbook.html

Machine Learning Repository. http://archive.ics.uci.edu/ml

Statistical Aspects of Data Mining (lecture taught by prof. Rajan Patel). http://www.youtube.com/watch?v=zRsMEl6PHhM

Cross Industry Standard Process for Data Mining. http://www.crisp-dm.org/

CHAPTER 5

Customer Intelligence

5.1. Introduction

In chapter 3, the application of information in sales and marketing was discussed, and in chapter 4, the business applications of advanced analysis were examined.

Traditionally, business intelligence (BI) analysis focused on an enterprise and its environment. People as a subject were not researched, unless as anonymous clients through their shopping habits. However, when clients began to be unambiguously identified and their behavior registered (e.g., in banking or telecom operators' billing systems), a close analysis of an individual client emerged. Analyses clustered mainly around analytical systems for client relationship management. The notable benefits resulting from close behavioral analysis of clients inspired similar solutions in Internet and mobile marketing, as well as in what is broadly understood as e-business.

The identification of an individual client enables the full application of the techniques of direct marketing (database marketing),[1] which is defined as directly interacting with a present or potential purchaser of the company's product. The revolutionary qualities that BI techniques introduced into direct marketing are as follows:

- Monitoring and full recording of a client's behavior patterns
- Application of advanced analytical techniques
- The chance to integrate data about the client that comes from different sources (i.e., information about transactions by credit cards along with information about his interests taken from social networks)

New telecommunication technologies related to potential constant access to a client by using mobile systems and access to information about the client's location provide additional possibilities.[2] As observed by Sean Kelly,[3] the marketing message profile (in accordance with the below-the-line, or BTL,[4] approach), which results from the departure from mass marketing (the above-the-line, or ATL,[5] approach), is based on one-to-one communication founded on BI techniques.

5.2 Customer Intelligence and Data Mining

The development of direct marketing along with the application of e-business and BI technologies resulted in the emergence of a subdiscipline of marketing based on client analysis, which is called customer intelligence (CI). One may interpret this as the analytical processing of data about a client for marketing purposes. This approach entails the collection, analysis, and use of data about a client. The client's behavioral history is investigated in order to determine his or her profile, preferences, and needs. This serves as the basis for the creation of a marketing message customized for a specific client. The main areas of support for marketing client analysis by BI techniques within CI are as follows:

1. The identification of potential clients (target group)
2. The selection of communication channels
3. The choice of a relevant message and time to convey it

Each of these areas may be supported by the application of data-mining methods. These techniques, which allow the possibility of classification, enjoy considerable popularity. It is possible to build precise models of either communication channel selection or the choice of the message itself. It is worth mentioning that there are methods that enable one to compute the correspondence between a real client profile (a de facto recognized profile) and the pattern profile of the client who is a purchaser of a given product. It permits one to carry out an efficient selection of clients and recipients of a given advertising campaign, and it delivers adequate results. The campaign is targeted at clients who correspond to the pattern profile (in the context of similarity measure).[6] The advertising campaign is then reviewed by a response model, which enables you to prove the hypothesis that there is a higher response from clients who are selected according to a correspondence with the pattern profile compared with clients selected at random.[7]

To illustrate the issues discussed, let us consider the following examples of their application:

1. *Selling cosmetics in perfume chain stores*
   - *Client identification.* It was determined that the client is keen on beauty care (information obtained from analysis of posts on the Internet forum), and her profile meets the requirements of the following pattern profile: sex = woman, and age = 25+.
   - *Channel of communication.* Short message service (SMS) or multimedia messaging service (MMS) can be used, depending on the model of the client's phone.
   - *Time of message.* The message can be transmitted when the client enters a shopping mall.
   - *Message.* The information will be about a special offer of a new line of cosmetics in a store located in a shopping mall.

2. *Selling of financial products by a retail bank*
   - *Client identification.* The pattern profile consists of clients with a high income, in managerial positions, age = 40+. Purchasers of cars make α model β were observed to have a corresponding profile. Thanks to an agreement with a car dealer of make α, access to the e-mail addresses of customers of model β was obtained.
   - *Channel of communication.* E-mail.
   - *Time of message.* Simultaneously with an invitation to join an enthusiast club for owners of car make α.
   - *Message.* Personalized offer of a long-term deposit account.

5.3. Personalization of the Marketing Message

The aforementioned examples are close to fulfilling a marketing manager's dreams, in which clients receive, at the right place and at the right time, a marketing message that is adjusted to their needs. Still, it is not an easy task, and badly targeted marketing messages are more usual:[8]

- *Untimely message.* A client is identified properly, but the message reaches him or her too late.
- *Irrelevant message.* A client is identified properly, but when he or she receives the message, he or she takes no interest in an offer.
- *Repeat message.* A client repeatedly receives the same message.
- *Unqualified message.* A message sent to a client is misunderstood; it may also happen that there is no chance to serve him or her when he or she responds positively.
- *Discordant message.* A message is relevant, but it is interwoven with other messages that are unsuitable, although they come from the same source.

A suitable marketing message should therefore

- correspond to a client's needs,
- correspond to a client's profile,
- be consistent with other marketing messages sent to a client,
- meet the client's requirements concerning obtained permission,
- be sent at the right time and in context the client understands,
- be sent in a manner that is most compatible with its content and the client's preferences,
- make a response easier for a client.

Both the content and form of a suitable marketing message are a consequence of a client's profile.[9] The profile itself is worked out on the basis of the data collected about a client. However, the data are not always collected directly, and in many cases they are collected when a client is unaware that a profile is being registered or deduced from previous data. In principle, collecting data about a client falls into one of four categories:[10]

- *Perfect data.* These are actual information registered through contact with a client, such as full name, address, and so on, which is obtained directly from a client when a contract with a client is being concluded.

- *Imperfect data.* Data that is unreliable because they are connected with a product or service that may be used by more than one person (i.e., prepaid mobile phones).
- *Passive data.* Data that are not provided consciously by a client but are registered by monitoring his or her behavior—that is, buying preferences registered when he or she conducts transactions by a credit card or client preferences determined on the basis of registration of so-called click streams (which are a sequence of visits to websites and registered keywords used in search engines). Yet another example is the determining of the intensity and the nature of social contacts on the basis of a contact map, which is built through analysis of telephone calls, traffic, and SMS content.[11]
- *Derived data.* Data about a client deduced informally from other data; for example, age might be concluded from registered interests or previous shopping. Obviously, such data has limited credibility.

5.4. On the Eve of Revolution

At present, telecom providers, banks, and so on build their own local and closed database about clients. A given client is registered individually in each of the systems, and these data are closely guarded (see example in Figure 5.1). Companies do not usually exchange these data with one another[12] due to legal restrictions (e.g., data protection), obligations to a client in the scope of confidentiality, the fear of losing clients, or legal claims due to data leakage.

Figure 5.2 shows hypothetical warehouse data about clients, where Ω is identified as a client:

- α in a cellular telecommunications provider A
- β in a retail bank B
- γ in an Internet social media portal C

Thanks to this integration, the data of a client's banking operations, telephone contacts, and social media activity are connected. What is most significant here is the synergy effect: the fact that we learn more from the

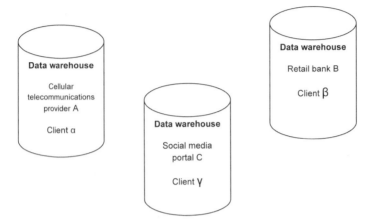

Figure 5.1. Local data warehouses—client data are stored independently.

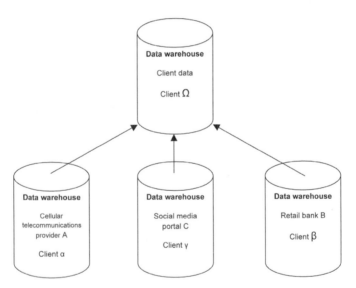

Figure 5.2. Client data integration in the one global warehouse.

two pieces of information combined than we would have learned from them individually.[13] Is the situation shown in Figure 5.2 possible at all?[14] Refraining from considering this issue from the formal and legal angle or in the context of works conducted by governmental institutions,[15] let us ponder it on a purely technically basis and consider the possible business consequences of such a solution. The idea of the registration of data connected from all aspects of an individual's life took shape in the MyLifeBits project.[16] Its author, Gordon Bell, formulated the concept of tracing events from the life of a specific person. These events can be stored on a computer and searched. The following events from a person's life could be registered:

- Written documents (e-mails, articles, notes, letters, blogs, bills, etc.)
- Viewed e-mails, newspapers, websites, studies, books, etc.
- Viewed photos, images, and posters
- Music (radio, CDs, MP3s, etc.)
- Movies
- All owned files
- All telephone calls and sent or received texts and MMS
- Shopping done
- Places visited
- Results of both periodic medical tests and day-to-day monitoring of one's pulse, body temperature, etc.

In the final phase of the project, it was even tested to see whether it would be possible to register all the events in a person's life by means of a head-mounted camera. Data warehouses with a large memory capacity, which are able to store the data provided for a person's whole life, are cheap and easily available. For a better understanding, let us consider two possible applications:

1. *Recommendation of an optimal diet and warnings of dangerous dietary practices on the basis of*
   - analysis of day-to-day monitoring and history of consumed products;
   - health;
   - availability of recommended products;
   - analysis of the diet and its results for people with similar health problems.
2. *Support for a high school graduate in selecting a university and major on the basis of*
   - evolution of interests;
   - ranking and kind of high school he or she graduated from;

- availability of universities and analysis of their graduates' careers;
- data about employment, demography, and forecasts about the developments of different sectors;
- career paths of people with similar career profiles.

All in all, the vision of a total-surveillance society in a totalitarian state ruled by Big Brother, as described in *Nineteen Eighty-Four* by George Orwell, is at present technically viable. However, the so-called paradox of privacy and confidentiality emerges.[17] There is a natural contradiction between clients' concerns about their privacy and their desire to receive messages that are adjusted to their needs. It is impossible to satisfy these two mutually opposite needs at the same time. Clients can consent to their personal data being processed and even support the process of building their profile if, for instance, they are given

- a possibility to sell their profile, for example, to companies that manage marketing databases for direct marketing purposes;
- special offers, bonuses, discounts, promotions, and so on;
- a high-quality personalized message in the area they are particularly interested in, provided that they have a guarantee that the information about them will remain confidential.

Google products may become an interesting platform for the application of customer intelligence techniques. Let us consider its business model and current solutions as an example of potential analytical possibilities. The basic business model provided by Google consists of offering Internet advertisement related to specific keywords. Therefore, these advertisements reach users by means of sponsored links, among other things, and Google matches their interests expressed by entries in the search engine.

As mentioned before, it is important for advertisers to adjust their marketing message to match the targeted user's profile. Therefore, the collection of information about clients enables Google to profile clients potentially very precisely. This should result in Google being able to offer advertisers numerous target groups that are interested in advertised products and services. One of the ways to achieve this could be to ensure

Internet users free access to a number of Internet applications. If registered users take advantage of such an offer and use the search engine, a notepad, blogs, and documents, it is possible to determine their interests, views, opinions, career profile, and so on, and then their contact groups and the nature of those personal contacts, business contacts, interests, and so on might be determined when they make use of discussion groups, e-mail, or calendars. Subsequently, it is highly probable to be able to determine age, sex, education, occupation, place of residence, income, and so on. Requiring an ID[18] to allow the client access to all the applications solves the problem of identifying a specific person. Giving one's ID plays a key role in, inter alia, linkage of a client's various activities.

As a result, personalized marketing activities as shown in Figure 5.3 become possible. The clients' activities can be monitored and their data stored in the data warehouse. Consequently, the history of clients' behavior is retained and their profile discovered. Such a profile is dynamic by nature and is updated after each activity at fixed intervals. The creation of the profile might be supported by BI methods. It's worth remembering that the cross- and upsell proposals for a given target group can make use of data-mining methods. Single profiles can be grouped accordingly, and that might be the basis for determining the regularity and rules for client segments. A lot of items in a profile are derived data, which means that this knowledge is unreliable. This is due to the fact that there is a great quantity of text data (i.e., blogs, e-mails, documents). It is essential to use text data-mining methods. The profile of a given client is the basis for the selection of an advertised product.[19]

In this context, virtual reality simulators such as Second Life[20] seem to be an interesting research laboratory. In such artificial worlds, total surveillance is possible, which translates into extremely precise profiling. Consequences for marketing are remarkable, but consequences for mankind are alarming.

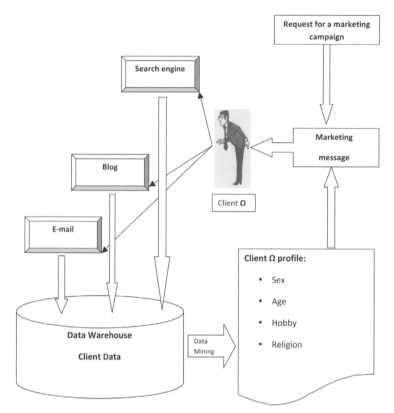

Figure 5.3. Possible architecture for targeting personal message in the integrated internet environment.

Source: author.

Recommended Literature

One-to-One Business

Kelly, S. (2006). *Customer intelligence: From data to dialogue.* New York, NY: Wiley.

Prahalad, C. K., & Krishnan, M. S. (2008). Analytics: Insight for innovation. In *The new age of innovation* (chap. 3). New York, NY: McGraw-Hill.

Understanding of Human Behavior Based on Digital Footprints

González, M. C, Hidalgo, C. A., & Barabási, A. L. (2008). Understanding individual human mobility patterns. *Nature, 453*, 479–482.

Lazer, D., et al. (2009). Life in the network: The coming age of computational social science. *Science 323*(6), 721–723.

Mitchell, T. M. (2009). Mining our reality. *Science, 326*(18), 1644–1645.

Petland, A. (2008). *Honest signals: How they shape our world.* Cambridge, MA: MIT Press.

Privacy, Futurology, and Popular Books

Attali, J. A. (2009). *Brief history of the future: A brave and controversial look at the twenty-first century.* New York, NY: Arcade Publishing.

Baker, S. (2008). *The numerati.* Boston, MA: Mariner Books.

O'Harrow, R. (2006). *No place to hide.* New York, NY: Free Press.

Solove, D. J. (2004). *The digital person: Technology and privacy in the information age.* New York, NY: New York University Press.

Internet Resources

Reality Mining Project. http://reality.media.mit.edu/

SocialNets. http://www.social-nets.eu/

SocioPatterns. http://sociopatterns.org/

Life Analytics Blog. http://lifeanalytics.blogspot.com/

Digital Footprints Mining. http://surma.edu.pl/

CHAPTER 6

Business Intelligence and Value-Based Management

6.1. The Role of Information Capital in Enhancing the Value of an Enterprise

The various technologies and applications of business intelligence (BI) described earlier all have the potential to enhance the value of an enterprise. However, this value is often only potential value and is therefore hard to quantify. In this chapter, this problem will be investigated at length by examining value-based management[1] and the current trends in management. Studies of the relationship between the use of business decision support systems and the value of an enterprise are quite complex, as information assets are intangible. This issue merits special attention because the proper selection and application of innovative technologies may considerably enhance the value of an enterprise.

6.1.1. Intangible Assets

Tangible assets, such as financial resources, can be easily indentified. They are the basis of financial analysis and are commonly accepted in determining the value of an enterprise. However, recent developments in business practices have led to an increased interest in determining the value of intangible assets. That is also how Robert Kaplan and Peter Norton's balanced scorecard concept emerged.[2] Business decision support systems are a part of information capital, which in turn is intangible. According to Kaplan and Norton, intangible assets fall into three categories that are essential for the realization of a company's strategy:

1. *Human capital.* Skills, abilities, and knowledge of employees.
2. *Organizational capital.* Organizational culture, quality of leadership, people's adjustment to strategic tasks, and their ability to share knowledge with others.
3. *Information capital.*

These resources are connected to the company's strategy by a strategy map (see Figure 6.1), and they belong to the learning and development perspective in the balanced scorecard. The realization of a strategy is supposed to enhance the value of an enterprise. A widely used method of determining the value of a company in the financial perspective is to work out its economic value added (EVA).[3] The strategy map, as an attempt to represent the sources of value in the enterprise, is an extension of the value chain concept from chapter 3. There are a few vital differences between determining the value of intangibles and tangible and financial assets:[4]

- *Indirect value creation.* Intangibles seldom have direct influence on financial results. They usually influence the finance of an enterprise by a complex chain of cause-and-effect relationships.[5] For instance, information capital has an impact on the decisive internal processes from the angle of creating value for customers, reducing the costs of realizing processes, or both. As a result, income growth, the reduction of operational costs, or both translate directly into the value of an enterprise, which is monitored by certain financial indicators grouped in the financial perspective.
- *Potential value.* The value of intangibles is potential—that is, it can be used to create the value of a company, but the investment itself in those assets does not make the value grow. Investment in intangibles that support internal processes but do not increase revenue from customers may even generate unexpected costs and reduce the value of the company.
- *Integration.* Intangibles hardly ever create value themselves, so they have to be integrated with other assets from the same perspective. For example, investments in information technology (IT) bring results only if they are integrated with training and suitable motivational programs for employees.[6]

- *Time.* The potential value chain generated by intangibles is strongly time dependent. The primary competitive advantage gained by the implementation of an innovative IT system may be rapidly lost if the competition imitates it. If intangibles are not properly managed, they may become outdated very fast, and that may have a negative influence on the value of an enterprise. The classic example is the implementation of an electronic ordering system by American Hospitals Supply, which initially generated superb financial results. However, after a few years, due to obsolete technology and the lack of modernization, it reduced the company's market position and hindered its development.[7]

6.1.2. Information Capital

Attitudes toward the use of IT such as BI in enterprises vary from an enthusiasm for IT to disappointment and harsh criticism. IT has become so ubiquitous that the services and products it produces have become almost invisible. An even stronger charge against IT is the argument that we are witnessing the twilight of the strategic value of IT systems.[8] Among

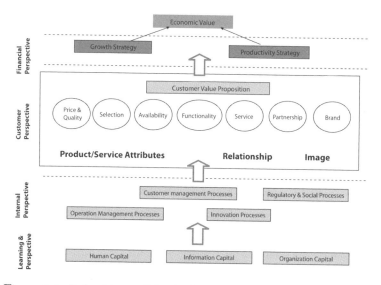

Figure 6.1. Role of intangibles in the strategy map.

Source: Based on Kaplan and Norton (2004).

such critical voices, Lester Thurow's reflection[9] seems to be particularly important, despite being somewhat overstated: "There are single cases, where new technologies contributed to production growth and reduction of costs. However, when it comes to more general statements, there is no unambiguous evidence that new technologies enhanced productivity and profitability." Such a firm conclusion is based on situations in which IT systems are implemented without being clearly linked to enhancing the value of the company. Having said this, it should be stressed that the failure to implement IT technologies properly does not automatically imply that they have no influence on the competitive advantage of a company. Instead, we should pay attention to the revolutionary impact of IT on the contemporary economy. Such criticism seems to emphasize how difficult it is to select, implement, and keep appropriate IT solutions up and running. The recent rapid development of IT systems implies countless classifications and attempts at their synthesis. Kaplan and Norton suggested the division of information capital, as is shown in Table 6.1. IT infrastructure allows for the application of two basic kinds of programs: transactional and analytical systems. Both can be the basis of transformation applications, which determine the business model of the company. Analytical applications—that is, BI systems—are information capital.

Case Study 6.1 shows a strategic map for a chain store.

Table 6.1. *Information Capital*

Category	Description
Transformation applications	Systems that modify and determine the business model of the enterprise.
Analytical applications	Systems that promote analysis, interpretation, and sharing of information and knowledge: business intelligence system.
Transactional systems	Systems making repeatable transactions that support the company's core business processes. The most popular examples in this group are IT management systems, ERP, or customer account banking systems. Technologically, such systems are constructed by database management systems and application servers, which ensure security and cohesion of online transaction processing (OLTP).
Technological infrastructure	Technologies (such as computer hardware and software), network infrastructure, and adequate security and quality standards, etc. They are necessary to use and keep IT applications up and running.

Source: Based on Kaplan and Norton (2004).

Case Study 6.1

Here is a fragment of the strategy map for the chain store ALFA (see figure 6.2), which was devised from the company's strategy (see Case Study 1.1), which includes the following:

- *From the perspective of learning and growth,* implementation of the managerial dashboard and application of data-mining methods
- *From the perspective of internal processes,* improvement of logistics processes, merchandising optimization, and cost control

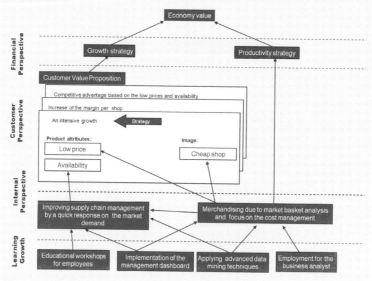

Figure 6.2. The ALFA chain store strategy map

Source: author.

6.2. Implementation Methodology

As mentioned before, even the most technologically sophisticated BI alone will not enhance the value of the company alone. It is crucial to connect it with the internal business processes of the company (see Figure 6.3) and take into account the organizational context and the human factor.[10] The implementation methodology of a BI system should then meet the following conditions:

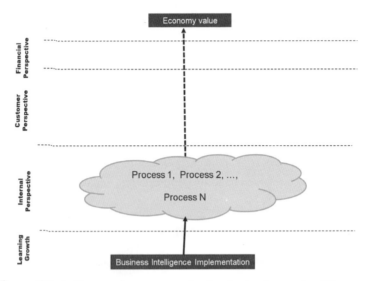

Figure 6.3. Indirect enhancement of value by implementing BI.

Source: author.

1. In the context of indirect and potential enhancement of value, it should employ business process reengineering[11] and should have a positive influence on the value of the company.[12]
2. As for the human capital and organizational context, it should relate to change management.

Meeting these conditions (see Figure 6.4) is a prerequisite for the successful implementation of a BI project. If you want to show the relationship

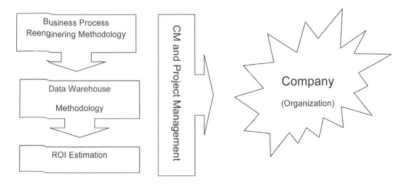

Figure 6.4. Holistic approach for the methodology of BI implementation.

Source: author.

to the economic value of the company, it is vital to adapt the whole to the strategy of the company and draw up clear-cut guidelines on the estimation of return on investment (ROI).[13] It should consist of two stages:

- Stage 1: Analysis (see Figure 6.5)
  - Phase 1: Reference to the strategy
  - Phases 2–3: Business processes reengineering
  - Phase 4: Recommendations
- Stage 2: Implementation (see Figure 6.6)
  - Phases 5–6: Implementation of recommendations
  - Phases 7–8: Use and analysis of ROI

The link between stages 1 and 2 (from phases 4 to 6) is the management board strategic decision to implement the BI solutions devised by reengineering of the business processes. In most cases, it will be the

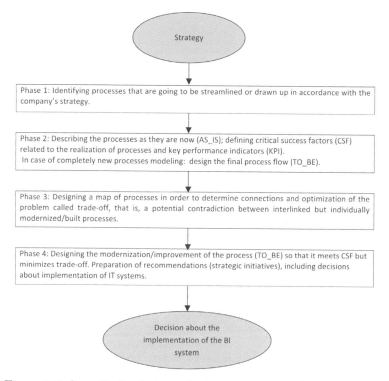

Figure 6.5. Stage 1: Analysis—referring to strategy and process reengineering.

Source: author.

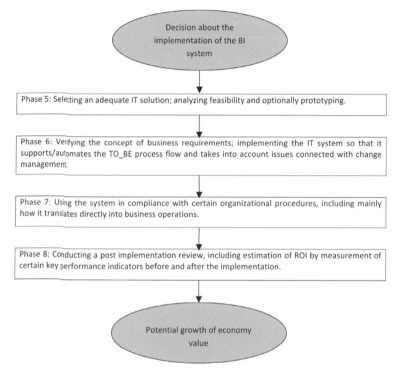

Figure 6.6. Stage 2: Implementation and use of the system.

Source: author.

implementation based on the data warehouse approach, as described in chapter 2. A review of the most common methods for implementing data warehouses can be found in O'Donnell's[14] and Adelman and Moss's[15] studies. The classic example is the SAS Rapid Methodology[16](see Figure 6.7). 6.8 shows how the results of the reengineering of business processes are transferred from the PROMET BPR methodology (from stage 1; see Figure 6.5) to the SAS Rapid Methodology (to stage 2; see Figure 6.6). If the system is designed to provide managerial information through online analytical processing (OLAP) tools, the integration is based on the following chain of connections:

strategy → processes → critical success factors (CSFs) → key performance
   indicators[17] → implementation of the managerial information system

If the implementation of the strategic initiative requires the use of advanced data-mining techniques, then for phase 6 (see Figure 6.6)

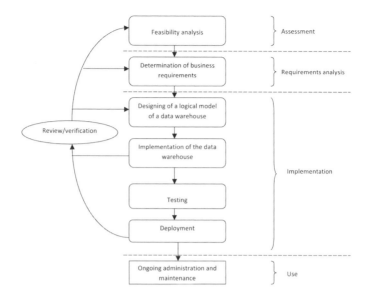

Figure 6.7. Stages of data warehouse designing.

Source: Based on SAS (2000).

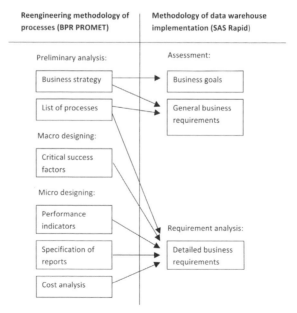

Figure 6.8. Linkage between the reengineering methodology of processes and the implementation methodology (PROMET BPR versus SAS Rapid Metholdogy).

Source: author.

you will have to use of the specialized methodology of data-mining methods (i.e., the cross-industry standard process for data mining, or CRISP-DM).[18] The transformation process from data in a data warehouse to potentially useful knowledge produced by means of CRISP-DM is shown in Figure 6.9 (see also chapter 4). It should be stressed that the aforementioned methodology (from reference to the strategy of the company to the evaluation of business profits from the BI implementation) is the most appropriate if the company has a clear-cut strategy. In such a strategy, business processes are identified first, and then the most suitable recommendations for BI application are matched to them. However, in practice, companies usually do not have a clear strategy for IT development, and investment decisions are made ad hoc, based on the principle "let's implement system x in department y."[19]

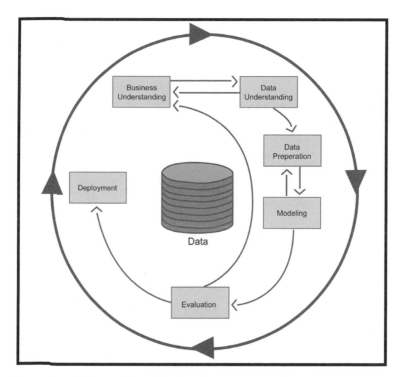

Figure 6.9. Phases of the CRISP-DM process model.

Source: http://www.crisp-dm.org/Process/index.htm

6.3. Levels of Support of Business Processes

IT systems support business processes by means of the following levels (see also chapter 3):[20]

- *Automation.* The process already exists, but it is automated, and parameters such as cost, time, and optionally quality and flexibility are improved.
- *Improvement.* The process already exists, but it is improved.
- *New process.* The process did not exist before.

Each level of support will be discussed in the context of the previously mentioned four standard critical success factors (CSFs): time (duration), cost, quality, and flexibility (see chapter 3).

6.3.1. Automation

Automation of a business process decreases duration and improves the quality of generated products. For an illustration of the effect of automation on reporting activities (in controlling process), see the description in Table 6.2 and the summary of business benefits in Table 6.3.

Examples of critical success factors for the automation of reporting are quicker reporting and its high value, which are measured by the following indicators, respectively: delivery time of the report and the number of errors (see Figure 6.10). Improvement of both indicators can be directly used to estimate the reduction of costs, which along with the implementation cost can serve as the basis for the financial assessment of this investment. However, from the businesses' point of view, the automation of the

Table 6.2. Example: Automation of the process.

Process	Automation of the sales results reporting in the controlling process
Sector	Distribution and trade
Description	Implementation of the online analytical processing (OLAP) reporting system, which uses data warehouses and replaces manually generated Excel reports. Table 6.3 shows potential benefits from transition from AS_IS (Excel) to improvement TO_BE (OLAP tools).

Source: author.

Table 6.3. Business Profits From the Automation of Reporting Processes

Process CSF	Potential profit
Cost	Less people involved in preparing the report → reduction of costs
Quality	Less errors, higher quality of data, more thorough drill-down analysis, better visualization → • More comprehensive knowledge about the business issue → potential influence on income growth • Avoidance of time-consuming error correction → reduction of costs
Time	Much less time spent on preparing the report → • Earlier knowledge about business events, more time for the analysis, or both → potential influence on income growth • Reduction of costs

Source: author.

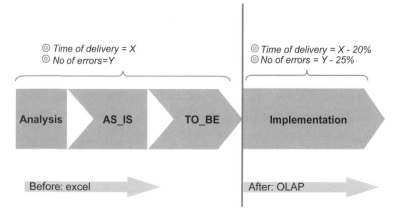

Figure 6.10. Example: Measurement of the automation of report preparation.

Source: author.

business process is the most obvious, but simultaneously the most dubious, way of using IT technologies. And then "the application of IT technology implies the automation of the process and consequently leads to its greater promptness. Automation of the process is the lowest level of change that can be accomplished through IT application."[21] The ROI can be controversially long, particularly if the implementation was costly, whereas the value added may seem to be hardly perceptible. Illustrative of this kind of BI application is the implementation of reporting systems in compliance with international accounting standards. In large corporations, the preparation of consolidated reports is likely to be such a time-consuming and onerous task that the automation itself of such a process, which allows for the reduction of the human capital involved and improvement of the quality of reports, should be a rational justification for the implementation.

6.3.2. Improvement

The improvement of a business process consists of the modification of either the process itself or the manner in which the tasks are performed. As a result, the process becomes more effective. Unlike the automation of the process, where generally the process and its products remain unchanged, in the case of improvement, the end result of the streamlined process can be much better. As the example of the OLAP system shows, the proper use of a new reporting system can also serve as an example of improvement, such as when a manager takes advantage of the analytical capacity that gives him a deeper understanding of business events (see Table 6.4). Another example of the improvement of a process is the modernization of the planning process (see the description in Table 6.5 and summary of business benefits in Table 6.6).

Table 6.4. Business Benefits From Improvement of the Sales Analysis Process

Process CSF	Potential benefit
Flexibility	Possibility to generate queries ad hoc and nonstandard analyses → • Additional knowledge about business events → potential influence on income growth • Quick preparation of additional report (e.g., by drilling down and rolling up) → reduction of costs

Source: author.

Table 6.5. Example: Improvement of the Process

Process	Improvement of the process of planning demand
Sector	Production and sales of fast-moving consumer goods
Description	Implementation of the system generating support for the process of sales forecasting (demand planning) by means of econometric forecasting techniques Table 6.6 shows the potential benefits from the transition from AS_IS (forecasting based on intuition and experience) to improved process TO_BE (making use of results of an econometric model)

Source: author.

Table 6.6. Business From Improvement of the Process of Demand Planning

Process CSF	Potential benefit
Cost	No direct reduction of the cost of planning the process
Quality	More precise forecasting → • Long production cycles → reduction of production costs • Less stores → reduction of storage costs • Minimization of out-of-stock items → income growth
Time	Much less time spent on generating a forecast → potential income growth
Flexibility	The taking into account of additional factors (e.g., promotions, modified past data) → reduction of costs, potential income growth, or both

Source: author.

The improvement of business processes is the most common way in which BI supports the management of a company to potentially enhance its value. In fact, almost all the examples of its application shown in chapter 3 (Tables 3.15, 3.16, 3.17, 3.18) and chapter 4 (e.g., Table 4.6) are related to the improvement of processes.

6.3.3. New Process

Innovation in an enterprise—that is, the implementation of cutting-edge IT solutions—may demand a new business process that will fit into the company's existing internal processes. Usually, this process does not exist yet because it cannot function effectively without IT systems. This is typical of IT-driven processes, the existence of which depends on IT. Let us consider this issue by examining the example of the implementation of a marketing campaign management system (see description in Table 6.7).

As opposed to automation and improvement, in this case, you cannot show the difference between AS_IS and TO_BE because AS_IS does not exist when you create a new process (see Figure 6.4). Therefore, it is not possible to directly show the reduction of costs. Instead, the whole investment analysis focuses on an estimation of potential income growth. Here investments are usually connected with the implementation of transformation applications. Let us additionally consider the example of using market basket analysis (see Figure 6.11) to show the estimation of ROI. You carry

Table 6.7. Example: New process.

Process	Marketing campaign management system in order to reduce the number of customers who leave to competitors (churn)
Sector	GSM telecommunications
Description	Implementation of the marketing campaign system targeted at customers who are likely to leave and go to their competitors. The identification and offering of the most appropriate service to such customers demand the application of advanced analysis and data-mining techniques on great volumes of data registered in the billing system. This cannot be put into practice without BI tools.

Source: author.

out comparative research—that is, you compare stores in which associations between products in a market basket are analyzed and adequate operations are performed with stores in which such actions have not been taken. You can calculate an average market basket for both the first and second groups and consequently estimate the ROI. This will be further discussed in section 6.4.

Those examples reflect the business process reengineering approach, according to which "the real power of technology is not about improvement

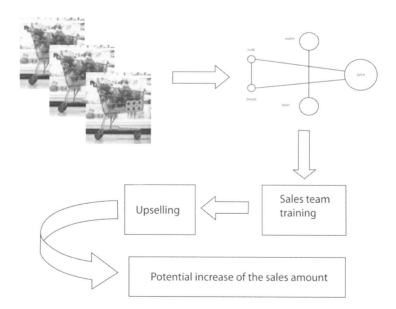

Figure 6.11. Analysis of the market basket as a new business process.

Source: author.

of old processes, but about enabling companies to give up old principles and create new ways of doing their work, that is reengineering."[22] That's why companies are often advised to use the process reference models implemented in IT systems (especially in enterprise resource planning systems) because they reflect the best business practices. These reference models are based on the experiences and knowledge of enterprises that participated in the implementation of earlier versions of the system. This is a kind of natural evolution of change in the organization during the implementation of an IT system, including BI implementation in particular.

6.3.4. Summary

There are three ways in which you can link BI with business processes: automation, improvement, and creation of a new process. It should be stressed that you can link BI with main (output), supporting, and managerial (controlling) processes, as they were defined in chapter 3. The last one plays a crucial role in BI applications, as they may be called metaprocesses, or processes that manage other processes. If you manage processes through key performance indicators (see chapter 3), you seem to naturally use BI tools. Although these days BI is normally used for controlling purposes,[23] the question of the cost of a controlling system versus the benefits of its implementation still needs to be addressed.

6.4. BI Implementation: Estimation of Return on Investment

The relationship between a company's value and the implementation of an IT system (including a BI system) may be proved if the implementation is interpreted as an investment project. If the potential increase of a company's value due to an investment project is measured by net present value (NPV), a direct relationship can be observed:

$$NPV > 0 \rightarrow \text{potential increase of company's value.}$$

We can talk here only about the potential increase of value because a concrete investment project does not exist in a vacuum. Quite the opposite, it shares resources with other processes and coexists with other investment projects. And that's why the project itself may be successful as an investment, but at the same time it may lead to losses in other areas (e.g., by key workers being overloaded with work), which result in a decrease in the company's value.

The financial interpretation of BI projects was first thoroughly discussed in an article by Steve and Nancy Williams.[24] From a financial point of view, the implementation of IT systems is a material investment, in which both basic and advanced profitability assessment methods can be employed. In practice, only basic methods are used: ROI, payback period, and discount methods, such as net present value, internal ROI, profitability ratio, and discount payback period. The interpretation of NPV is shown in Figure 6.12; the investment cost is in following years compensated by discount cash flows. The main problem with using financial investment assessment methods is the necessity to forecast the effect on the cash flow by a given investment. Such forecasts by definition have a wide margin of error. Positive cash flow can be generated by reducing costs (as in the example of a reporting system), and cash flow is relatively easy to estimate in the case of IT investments. However, cash flow resulting from profit growth (as in the example of a profit forecasting system) is extremely difficult to estimate. The profit growth depends on a combination of many factors that influence it at the same time. It is a highly complex issue to formally single out which of those factors increased profit and measure their share in the profit growth.

Another problem is an attempt to formalize factors that cannot be measured. As the example of an OLAP system shows (see Table 6.4), the accurate use of a new reporting system may give a manager a deeper

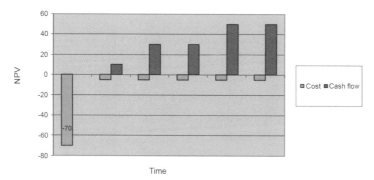

Figure 6.12. Calculation of NPV.

Source: author.

business insight. Let us assume that a sales manager finds out the next day rather than one week later about an unexpected growth in sales of a given product. Are we able to estimate the value of such information obtained a few days earlier? If adequate operations are performed, we may reduce so-called lost sales. And here the problem emerges of how we can measure the value of information. Let us consider the most vital problems that have an influence on the value that is attached to information:

1. *Amount.* The classic measurement of the amount stems from information theory (Claude Shannon's definition) and is based on entropy, which is of no use in business applications. In economic terms, the amount of information (value) should refer to practical value based on the extent to which it can satisfy human needs or to exchange value, that is, the possibility to exchange information for other goods.

2. *Accessibility.* The value of information decreases when an increasing number of people have access to it.

3. *Credibility of the source.* The value of information depends on the credibility of a provider.

4. *Usability.* The value of the information increases if a recipient can use it for practical purposes.

5. *Quality.* There is a relationship between the value of information and its quality, that is, whether a given message is true and complete.

6. *Context.* Experimental research proves that the subjective value of the information is subject to an endowment effect,[25] in which the value of a good in a salesperson's eyes is higher than in a purchaser's eyes.

7. *Life cycle.* The value of information depends on the time within which it is delivered to a user. Outdated information is usually worthless.

8. *Possible applications.* Information is of greater value if the same information can be simultaneously used by different people in an organization in different ways.

9. *Information symmetry or asymmetry.* It is a paradox that unless a purchaser obtains the given information, he or she does not know its content, but when it is revealed, he or she may not be interested in paying for it. It refers to the thesis according to which information

is an experience good, which means that it can be discovered exclusively through use.[26]

Economic models, which deal with difficult but significant problems, are still in the pipeline; here David Lawrence's monograph is recommended.[27]

6.5. Change Management and the Role of Human Capital

To measure the NPV, you naturally assume a certain ideal situation in which the implementation of an IT system is chosen wisely and is effectively used in a company. However, in practice, it too often happens that even the most appropriate decisions concerning technological implementation designed to enhance the company's value may turn out to be completely unwise if they are not effectively integrated with business processes, are rejected by users, or both. Technologies have to be accurately employed in order to support a concrete business process and should take into account the human factor; this is change management. As we know, intangibles hardly ever enhance the value of a company by themselves. They usually have to be combined with other assets from the same perspective. Reality often proves this thesis, and adequate change management is fundamental to the successful implementation of IT systems that support management. The implementation of IT systems based on useful project management know-how is now something obvious, but it is not enough to attain the final aim of the enhancement of a company's value. And that's why it is so important to manage change properly. In practice, this issue is usually ignored or treated intuitively without any methodological background. Change management aims to support the systematic human aspects and other critical factors for the success of the project, such as top executive support, team management, assessment of participants, and a proper communication between them. Participants are groups or people from within and without a company who have a direct influence on the project's advance, are under its direct or indirect influence, or both. Table 6.8 shows the tool designed to identify the participants and the relationships between them according to the PROMET Change Management methodology of the IMG company. The issue described in this chapter is combining information capital with human and organizational capital—that is, the specific psychology of the implementation and use of IT systems. Users should perceive this implementation as added value resulting from the BI tool's usability, prestige, personal development, interest in technology, and so on. This issue may particularly gain importance in the future, when IT systems begin to directly influence managerial decisions.

The proper "immersion" of IT in an organization means the complete symbiosis with human and organization capital in terms of learning and development perspective of the balanced scorecard. In this context it is important to discover adequate CSFs. Here, apart from basic indicators such as quality, time, and cost (see CSF 1–2 in Table 6.9), "soft" indicators emerge concerning business applications and the users' involvement (see CSF 3-4 in Table 6.9).

Finally, it should be stressed that a decision maker should refer to the company's strategy by making use of a strategy map that indirectly connects the investments in IT technologies with the strategic aims of the company. First of all, it is fundamental to understand how the company's

Table 6.8. Tools for Identifying Participants of the Project

Document	Description
List of participants	It describes the roles and functions of participants.
Map of participants	It shows the roles of participants and the relationships between them. It serves also as a system of early warning against potential sources of conflict.
Relationships between participants	It describes what the relationships between the participants on the map are.
Matrix of opportunities and threats	It shows potential threats and opportunities for each of the participants. It should be verified after each stage.
Diagram of project environment	It shows how the participants and other factors, such as resources and other projects, influence the project and contribute to its success.
Communication strategy	It describes the information that must be exchanged between the participants and tools that facilitate it. The main aims of the communication strategy are • well-developed information policies, • involvement of all target groups, • communication tools optimization, • smooth information exchange.

Source: Based on PROMET (1997).

*Table 6.9. Demonstration of the CSFs and KPIs for the
Implementation and Maintenance of IT Systems*

CSF	KPI
1. Proper realization of business requirements	• Percentage of proper realization of user requirements • Results of quality control tests
2. Effective use of budget and accessibility of the system in the accurate time	• Percentage of budget spending relative to project advance (earned value)
3. Understanding and full use by business users	• Ratio of users who work in reality to allocated ones • Number of successfully done trainings • Amount of use of nonstandard functions
4. Satisfaction of end users	• Questionnaire results

Source: author.

value is enhanced, but it also may show competition between departments and this "office politics" may be to the detriment of a department or to the business as a whole. This was previously mentioned as a trade-off problem in classic nonprocess organizations. Real life shows that building an effective strategy map is extremely difficult, particularly in the context of development and internal processes. And that's why presidents of companies usually follow their intuition when making fundamental and far-reaching decisions, whereas the strategy map and NPV estimations only support strategic business decisions.

6.6. Conclusions

At present, the application of BI systems and their influence on the enhancement of a company's value are not simply the subject of academic deliberations. These systems are employed in many companies, and in some cases they decide their competitive advantage. Indeed, you can compete by using cutting-edge BI techniques. Thomas Davenport and Jeanne Harris's book[28] summarizes several years of observations and research in that respect in the American market. According to the authors, a company that competes against others by using analysis is an organization that has one or more distinct capacities on which its strategy is based. As a result, it uses advanced analytical techniques of both quantitative and qualitative data and decision-making systems to support these capacities. A unique example of such an approach is Netflix, a mail-based DVD rental company.[29]

In conclusion, BI systems can have a positive influence on a company's value by supporting managerial decisions when you reasonably take into account the following factors:

1. Indirect enhancement of a company's value. BI systems are potentially able to generate business value through a complex chain of cause-and-effect relationships, from the learning and development perspective to the financial perspective.

2. Accurate integration of BI systems with business processes. Real life proves that even accurate decisions about implementation of BI systems, which should theoretically enhance a company's value, may turn out to be poor if those systems are not properly integrated with business processes.

3. The human factor and accurate change management. These help to properly combine the technological aspect of implementation with human and organizational capital.

4. Effective selection of key performance indicators, which allows for reliable business processes management and consequently reliable estimation of the ROI.

5. Difficulty with the estimation of the value of managerial information, which is quite often the main value of BI systems. This may result in an underestimation of the ROI if only measurable factors are considered.

The last case study shows a relationship map of the participants in a BI implementation project and some of the project's problems.

Case Study 6.2

A pilot strategic project (initiative), an analysis of a shopping basket, brought excellent results. Consequently, the project was implemented across the whole chain of Alfa stores. However, it met with such strong emotional reactions in the company that a professional change management was required in this area. An external consultancy company devised a map of the key participants of the project (e.g., marketing and sales manager, regional managers) and the relationship between them (see Figure 6.13).

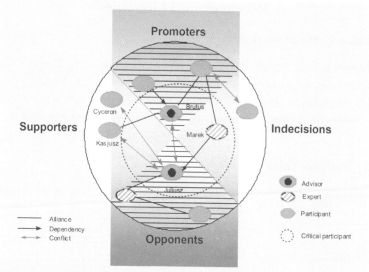

Figure 6.13. The key participants map

Source: PROMET (1997).

As real conflicts and resistance from some managers were discovered, training sessions were conducted and the results of the pilot project were presented. It turned out that some of these doubts stemmed from disbelief that analytical results (association rules) could be translated into the real activities of a store. To address this real threat and to be in line with the project methodology, which requires the integration of the BI system with business processes, a number of changes were made.

This new process aimed to generate additional sales through cashiers' activities, who, having observed the content of a given shopping basket, should offer additional products (see Figure 6.11). The manual for cashiers was prepared so that they would know exactly how to behave. Formally, the whole process was designed in accordance with an event-driven process chain[30] (EPC), in which all functions in the process, people who perform the functions, and events were described. One of the main deliverables of the whole process was the manual for the sales staff. In addition, the sales staff was thoroughly trained off-site. During this training, the whole process, including the way the manual was devised and the statistical grounds for it, was presented. Furthermore, a rewards system was introduced to motivate the sales staff to take advantage of the new approach.

Recommended Literature

Value-Based Management

Kaplan, R. S., & Norton, D. P. (2004). *Strategy maps: Converting intangible assets into tangible outcomes.* Boston, MA: Harvard Business School Press.

Martin, J. D., & Petty, J. W. (2000). *Value-based management: The corporate response to the shareholder revolution.* Oxford, UK: Oxford University Press.

BI Business Value

Williams, S., & Williams, N. (2006). *The profit impact of business intelligence.* San Francisco, CA: Morgan Kaufmann.

IT Business Value

Kohli, R., & Devaraj, S. (2002). *The IT payoff: Measuring the business value of information technology investments.* Upper Saddle River, NJ: Financial Times Press.

Weill, P., & Ross, J. W. (2004). *IT governance.* Boston, MA: Harvard Business School.

Weill, P., & Ross, J. W. (2009). *IT savvy.* Boston, MA: Harvard Business School.

Business Process Management and Reengineering

Hammer, M., & Champy, J. (2003). *Reengineering the corporation: A manifesto for business revolution.* New York, NY: Harper Paperbacks.

Jeston, J., & Nelis, J. (2008). *Business process management* (2nd ed.). London, UK: Butterworth-Heinemann.

Project Management

Cadle, J., & Yeates, D. (2007). *Project management for information systems* (5th ed.). Upper Saddle River, NJ: Prentice Hall.

Internet Resources

Value Based Management Net. http://www.valuebasedmanagement.net/
Project Management Institute. http://www.pmi.org/
Executive Strategy Manager. http:// www.executivestrategymanager.com/

Conclusion

Veritas est adaequatio rei et intellectus.

—Thomas Aquinas

In conclusion, the following are some thoughts on the current trends in the development of business intelligence (BI). There are two main trends in BI development: BI in Business-to-Customer (B2C) applications, and BI in enterprise management.

The direct marketing applications discussed in chapter 5 belong to the intriguing area of cutting-edge BI applications in B2C. It is even more important if you bear in mind that the trend that combines personalized marketing with analytical applications in mobile services is currently developing. There are four principal areas:

1. *Media convergence.* This refers to the personalization of access to standardized media in mobile devices. Examples are radio, television, the press, telephone, and the Internet in a portable device, in which a strictly personalized program or message is interlinked with a customized advertisement.

2. *Web mining and textual data analysis.* This refers to the analysis of users' behavior in Internet portals and social networks. Nowadays a wide range of analytical methods are used to analyze the web[1] and social networks.[2] This is possible because of the development of the text data-mining methods[3] described in the section devoted to strategic information (3.2.3). The semantic interpretation of social networks and the web is also very interesting. The development of the Semantic Web[4] allows for making queries in a natural language and generating additional knowledge by suitable reasoning systems. Intensive research is currently being undertaken despite the rather questionable achievements of Douglas Lenat's pioneering works in the CYC project.[5]

3. *Spatial location systems: geographical information system (GIS).* Finding correspondences between customers' behaviors and their location

is one of the dominant development trends mentioned in chapter 5. However, the location of the client also refers to the analysis of sales combined with information about the geographical arrangement of different segments of customers. This area of BI applications is developing rapidly and is particularly intriguing in the context of the development of data exploration methods representing spatial relations.[6]

4. *Virtual world.* This is one of the most fascinating trends in the development of personalized media and advertising. In the optimistic version, it would mean, among other things, solving Turing's test.[7] This is a situation in which a computer makes a dialogue in a natural language in such a way that its interlocutor is not able to recognize that he or she is talking to a "machine." Although a remedy for this problem has not been found yet, it should not inhibit the development of simulators of virtual worlds (e.g., Second Life). In the Second Life world, the problem of intelligence was solved by involving people in the process. The business context here is the capacity to build personalized advertising systems, which was mentioned in chapter 5.

In enterprise management, there is an evident tendency to depart from single ("point") solutions and turn to a holistic approach. Consequently, integrated information technology (IT) systems are built to support enterprises as a whole in terms of cost optimization, profits analysis, and forecasting and identification of opportunities and threats in the market environment. From this perspective, BI should not be an independent field anymore. It must become an integral component of the functionality of IT that supports management in a 21st-century enterprise. Nowadays, the research focuses on BI systems not only supporting decisions but also making decisions directly. Decision making consists of integrating results generated by the analysis of BI systems with directly operational managerial decisions (golden loop) and intelligent activation of activities on the basis of monitoring of events.

And now a final digression about the potential application of BI to solve ill-structured problems (Herbert Simon's classification from chapter 1). This category of ill-structured problems includes decisions that cannot be programmed and that concern new cases in which a common code of conduct does not exist and consequences are unpredictable. In chapter 3, it was suggested that you may support solutions to these kinds of problems by rationalization, that is, by providing the enterprise's board of directors with suitable strategic information. Another issue is what a manager does with this information and what his or her final decisions are. This is one of the most fascinating and vital trends in contemporary management, but it is not covered in this book. These problems have been the subject of intensive work as a part of research into artificial intelligence for over 50 years now.[8] The theories of uncertain knowledge representation, approximate reasoning systems, or practical natural language processing still rarely find their way from laboratory research to the real business world. Honest reflection on human thinking and reasoning leads to the conclusion that there is a huge gap between formal logic, which is a basis of automatic reasoning systems, and true human behavior. The present stage of the development of artificial intelligence shows that there is an obvious crisis in this area, and there are problems with using formal logic as a science in principles of reasoning. I think that ill-structured problems, which are sometimes analyzed within strong artificial intelligence, still cannot be truly supported by information technology.

Notes

Chapter 1

1. Newell and Simon (1972).

2. It is not widely known that the spectacular market success of Wal-Mart supermarkets also has its roots in the pioneering implementation of BI. Obviously, every chain follows the principle of "the right product at the right place, time, and price." Theoretically speaking, it is very simple, but it turns out to be incredibly difficult when it comes to realization. In practice, one tries to minimize costs connected with a logistics chain from a manufacturer's storehouse to a customer's basket by means of a manager's intuition rather than by any formal analyses. This chain is influenced by thousands of factors, such as season, fashion, region, price, and promotions, to name just a few. Wal-Mart was the first chain of supermarkets that had already started in the 1980s to electronically register events in the whole chain and aggregate them in a data warehouse. The conclusions drawn from a history of sales allowed the chain to globally reorganize logistics and reduce costs. This led to low prices that destroyed competitors (Westerman, 2000).

3. Inmon (2005).

4. The phrase "business intelligence" was introduced in Luhn (1958).

5. Gartner (2003).

6. Management IT systems fall into three generations: first-generation transaction systems, second-generation management information systems and data retrieval, and third-generation support systems, including BI ones (Kisielnicki, 2008).

7. Davenport and Harris (2007).

8. Simon (1977).

9. This is sometimes called a *golden loop*. A proposal of a solution from the BI system goes straight to the source system (the transaction one) as a parameter. For instance, in a company that manufactures chocolates for a storehouse, demand forecast generated by the analytical system automatically becomes a parameter. One can, on the basis of this parameter, determine both an order to suppliers and a manufacturing plan.

10. The analyses in the chart are usually based on information about sales or daily orders in a shop. However, sometimes the analysis is so detailed that it requires the consideration of data from single-till receipts (e.g., market basket analysis), but a buyer still remains anonymous. Loyalty programs introduced into

some chain stores are a new value in this respect because they link the "market basket" with a certain customer. Having this information enables businesses to make planned and precisely targeted marketing campaigns, which help retain present customers and attract new ones.

Chapter 2

1. OLTP provides solutions for operational activities of a company, such as effective and safe data storage, transaction data reconstruction, updating of data, optimization of the access to the data, and concurrency control (Garcia-Molina, Ullman, & Widom, 1999).

2. Inmon (2005).

3. Garcia-Molina, Ullman, and Widom (2008).

4. See http://www.inmoncif.com/

5. Codd, Codd, and Salley (1993), p. 7.

6. This fact table is used here for purely illustrative purposes, as "Costs" represents a very high level of aggregation, which in practice does not exist at the level of a fact table.

7. This table with the dimension "Date" is used here for purely illustrative purposes, as the lowest level of representation of time at the level of a month does not exist in practice.

8. For the definition of a primary key, see Ullman and Widom (2007).

9. For the definition of a foreign key, see Ullman and Widom (2007).

10. This class of technological systems is built by means of database management systems, which ensure suitable security and cohesion of data processing (OLTP).

11. Todman (2001).

12. Kimball and Ross (2002).

13. All schemas are simplified and solely illustrative.

Chapter 3

1. The term "OLAP" is variously understood by software producers. Some associate it directly with the physical organization of data in a data warehouse, whereas others refer to it as tools that are designed for business reporting. Those tools are integrated into the data warehouse, sometimes even directly into the source systems, and have their own built-in data storage mechanisms. In this book, this term is used in reference to tools devised for business reporting and analysis, which are integrated with the properly designed and optimized data warehouse.

2. Codd, Codd, and Salley (1993).

3. http://www.olapreport.com/fasmi.htm.

4. This book does not discuss the implementation of star schema in various data models, which are called ROLAP, MOLAP, and HOLAP. For further details, see the recommended literature.

5. This is a data description language, according to the terminology of database management systems.

6. This is a data manipulation language, according to the terminology of database management systems.

7. In general, aggregation might be done by sum, average, count, and so on.

8. Formally, hierarchies within dimensions are modeled by so-called snowflakes.

9. Stoner, Freelman, and Gilbert (1995).

10. Stefanowicz (2007).

11. It is connected with the Aristotelian concept of hylomorphism, in which he assumes that a being consists of matter (gr. *hyle*, or "material") and form (gr. *morph*, or "shape").

12. Strategic management is usually defined as a process that consists of three stages (Johnson, Scholes, & Whittington, 2008): analysis (the strategy position), planning (strategy choices), and implementation (strategy in action). In such a context, strategic information encompasses support for strategic analysis and planning; monitoring of strategy implementation will be discussed in reference to managerial information (balanced scorecard).

13. Stefanowicz (2007).

14. Porter (1998).

15. Hammer and Champy (2003).

16. Rummler and Brache (1995).

17. Franceschini, Galetto, and Maisano (2007). A comprehensive review of KPI can be found in Parameter (2007).

18. An example of a process event monitor is available at http://www.ids-scheer.com/

19. Giarratano and Riley (2004).

20. See, for instance, the supply chain operations reference (SCOR) model at http://supply-chain.org/

21. Silverstone (2001).

22. Kaplan and Norton (1996).

23. Kaplan and Norton (1996).

24. Obłój (2007).

25. Simon (1997).

26. Johnson, Scholes, and Whittington (2008).

27. Fuld (1994).

28. Tyson (2002).

29. Fuld (1994).

30. According to Fulleborn and Meier (1999), "The problem does not lie in the lack of information, but in the lack of time that a manager would have to devote to the analysis of all available data . . . Therefore, the primary goal of strategic information systems should not be providing information, but its filtering."

31. Look at the weak signal approach in strategy management (Day & Schoemaker, 2006).

32. Feldman and Sanger (2006).

Chapter 4

1. Hand, Mannila, and Smyth (2001).

2. Frawley, Piatetsky-Shapiro, and Matheus (1992); Piatetsky-Shapiro, Fayyad, Smyth, and Uthurusamy (1996).

3. Hand, Mannila, and Smyth (2001).

4. Larose (2004).

5. Aczel (2005).

6. Breiman, Friedman, Olshen, and Stone (1984).

7. Quinlan (1993).

8. This example is inspired by the Golf example from Quinlan (1993).

9. Quinlan (1993).

10. You can find further formulas and details concerning these calculations, among others things, in Quinlan (1993) and Larose (2004).

11. Larose (2004); Weiss and Kulikowski (1991).

12. Popper (2004).

13. Mitchel (1997).

14. Classification accuracy = the number of properly classified examples in the test set = (40 + 30) ÷ 100 = 0.7.

15. Anderberg (1973).

16. MacQueen (1967); Hartigan and Wong (1979).

17. Rószkiewicz (2002).

18. This approach was presented officially for the first time at the 1993 SIGMOD conference (Agrawal, Imielinski, & Swami, 1993).

19. One of the first business projects within this field was created by T. Blischoka from Terradata. Bills from 90 days were examined for a chain of 50 stores. At that time, it was discovered that on Friday afternoons there is a strong relationship between sales of beer and diapers.

20. In order to make this example simple, we assumed that juice, bread, milk, water, and beer are not product categories but specific product names.

21. Normally, there is also a third parameter: lift.

22. You can find a complete description of association rules analysis a priori in Larose (2004).

23. It is possible if you put additional virtual elements, such as a store identifier, data of the transaction, and so on, into the basket.

24. Consider, for example, "Customers Who Bought This Item Also Bought . . ." on Amazon.com.

25. For example, if there are 100 product indexes, the number of possible combinations of three products necessary for generating association rules is 167,700.

26. Hertz, Krogh, and Palmer (1991).

27. Michalewicz (1996).

Chapter 5

1. Nash (2000).

2. It is possible thanks to, inter alia, mobile communications, GPS, or identification and localized systems with the use of RFID.

3. Kelly (2006).

4. BTL advertising activities are targeted at a specific customer and are not advertised in the mass media. BTL advertising media are targeted mainly at retailers and consumers. Direct mail and consumer promotion belong to the BTL category.

5. ATL marketing activities occur in the traditional areas of the mass media, such as radio, the press, posters, and external advertisements.

6. There is extensive literature on similarity measures, which refer to nearest-neighbor methods within pattern recognition algorithms. See Duda, Hart, and Stork (2000). For cluster analysis, Anderberg (1973). For case-based reasoning, see Aamodt and Plaza (1994).

7. Berry and Linoff (2004). The example of mining social networks for marketing responses is in Surma and Furmanek (2010).

8. Kelly (2006).

9. This issue is connected with business psychology, where various methods are used (e.g., a psychological picture of a given customer profile is built up and then the proper marketing message can be devised).

10. U.S. Fair Trade Commission (2000).

11. See the example of inferring social network structure using mobile phone data in Eagle, Pentland, and Lazer (2009).

12. There are agreements between companies on the exchange of information about customers (e.g., about debts, credits).

13. For instance, say we are interested in a person Ω and in the activities of a foundation called "Bright Future" (recorded on an Internet portal in time t), a payment into the account of the foundation (registered by a bank in $t + 1$), and a visit in Boston (registered by mobile communications operator in $t + 2$). One can provisionally conclude that at the time $t + 2$, the person under study participated in a meeting of the members of the foundation's management board in Boston.

14. The global interactive marketing company Acxiom (http://www.acxiom.com) is a good example of approaching this business model.

15. It seems that there is no chance to move away from building government information systems, which follow this trend.

16. See http://research.microsoft.com/barc/MediaPresence/MyLifeBits.aspx and representative papers such as Gemmel, Bell, and Lueder (2006).

17. Kelly (2006).

18. It is possible to use less precise identification methods based on the records of identification data on a customer's PC (cookies).

19. This issue was officially addressed by Google on August 8, 2008: http://googlepublicpolicy.blogspot.com/2008/08/google-responds-to-congressional-letter.html. See also interest-based advertising (http://google.com/ads/preferences) and http://googleblog.blogspot.com/2009/03/making-ads-more-interesting.html

20. See http://secondlife.com/

Chapter 6

1. Rappaport (1986)

2. Kaplan and Norton (1996). A balanced scorecard is often implemented as a tool to realize an enterprise's strategy by means of BI tools. See chapter 3.

3. Look at Aswath Damodaran's explanation, available at http://www.pages.stern.nyu.edu/~adamodar/New_Home_Page/lectures/eva.html

4. Surma (2008).

5. Weil (1998).

6. Kaplan and Norton (2004).

7. Carr (2003).

8. Carr (2003).

9. Thurow (1991).

10. Williams and Williams (2003).

11. Bach, Brecht, Hess, and Osterle (1996); Osterle, Winter, Back, and Brenner (2004).

12. All examples refer to the engineering methodology of business processes of PROMET BPR drawn up by St. Gallen University (PROMET, 1997).

13. Williams and Williams (2006).

14. O'Donnell, Arnott, and Gibson (2002).

15. Adelman and Moss (2000).

16. SAS (2000).

17. The indicator will be interpreted as a measure in the modeling of a data warehouse described in chapter 2.

18. Larose (2004).

19. This approach is in many cases pretty rational, but it increases the risk of an enterprise losing value.

20. These levels of support can be employed for any kind of business process.

21. Lech (2003), p. 51.

22. Hammer and Champy (2003).

23. See the management of business processes in chapter 3.

24. Williams and Williams (2003).

25. http://www.endowment-effect.behaviouralfinance.net

26. Shapiro and Varian (1998).

27. Lawrence (1999).

28. Davenport and Harris (2007).

29. Netflix is based on a very simple business model: A monthly subscription allows customers to rent an unlimited number of films without any extra costs as long as they return previously rented movies. Customers can contact the company only via its web page, and movies are delivered to the customers by mail. The secret of the spectacular success of this company consists of perfect operational use of two analytical applications. The first is Cinematch, which is an automatic system of movie recommendations, which on the basis of a given customer's rental history and analysis of rentals of similar customers generates a list of recommended movies. Simultaneously, the system controls stock and does not display any unavailable items on the list of recommended movies. The second application was the algorithm"throttling," which is supporting the Netflix business model. If a customer pays a fixed monthly fee and does not cover any delivery costs, the best customer is one who seldom rents movies. This algorithm involved deciding which customers will be served most effectively and prioritizes the order of deliveries in such a way that the most active customers (i.e., the least profitable ones) are served last (http://en.wikipedia.org/wiki/Netflix). However, eventually Netflix officially rejected this algorithm.

30. http://en.wikipedia.org/Wiki/Event-driven_process_chain

Conclusion

1. Linoff and Berry (2002).

2. Wasserman and Faust (2009).

3. Feldman and Sanger (2006).

4. Antoniou and Harmelen (2008).

5. http://www.cyc.com/

6. Han and Kamber (2006).

7. http://www.turing.org.uk/turing/scrapbook/test.html.

8. Russel and Norvig (2009).

References

Aamodt, A., & Plaza, E. (1994). *Case based reasoning: Foundational issues, methodological variations, and system approaches* (Vol. 7). AI Communications. IOS Press.

Aczel, A. (2005). *Complete business statistics* (6th ed.). New York, NY: McGraw-Hill.

Adelman, S., & Moss, L. (2000). *Data warehouse project management.* Boston, MA: Addison Wesley.

Agrawal, R., Imielinski, T., & Swami, A. (1993). Mining association rules between sets of items in large databases. *Proceedings of the 1993 ACM SIG-MOD International Conference on Management of Data*, 207–216.

Anderberg, M. (1973). *Cluster analysis for applications.* New York, NY: Academic Press.

Antoniou, G., & Harmelen, F. (2008). *A semantic web primer* (2nd ed.). Cambridge, MA: MIT Press.

Bach, V., Brecht, L., Hess, T., & Osterle, H. (1996). *Enabling systematic business change: Integrated methods and software tools for business process redesign.* Braunschweig, Germany: Vieweg.

Berry, M. J., & Linoff, G. S. (2004). *Data mining techniques: For marketing, sales, and customer relationship management.* New York, NY: Wiley.

Breiman, L., Friedman, J., Olshen, R., & Stone, C. (1984). *Classification and regression trees.* Belmont, CA: Wadsworth International.

Carr, N. (2003, May). IT doesn't matter. *Harvard Business Review, 5*.

Codd, E. F., Codd, S. B., & Salley, C. T. (1993). *Providing OLAP user-analysts: An IT mandate.* San Jose, CA: Codd & Associates.

Daum, J. (1999). *The new generation of analytic applications to support management processes: Strategic enterprise management.* SAP AG.

Davenport, T. H., & Harris, J. G. (2007). *Competing on analytics.* Boston, MA: Harvard Business School Press.

Day, G. S., & Schoemaker, P. J. (2006). *Peripheral vision: Detecting the weak signals that will make or break your company.* Boston, MA: Harvard Business School Press.

Duda, R. O., Hart, P. E., & Stork, D. G. (2000). *Pattern classification.* New York, NY: Wiley-Interscience.

Eagle, N., Pentland, A., & Lazer, D. (2009). Inferring social network structure using mobile phone data. *Proceedings of the National Academy of Sciences (PNAS), 106*(36), 15274–15278.

Feldman, R., & Sanger, J. (2006). *Text mining handbook: Advanced approaches in analyzing unstructured data.* Cambridge, UK: Cambridge University Press.

Franceschini, F., Galetto, M., & Maisano, D. (2007). *Management by measurement: Designing key indicators and performance measurement systems.* Berlin, Germany: Springer Verlag.

Frawley, W., Piatetsky-Shapiro, G., & Matheus, C. (1992, Fall). Knowledge discovery in databases: An overview. *AI Magazine.*

Fuld, L. (1994). *The new competitor intelligence: The complete resource for finding, analyzing, and using information about your competitors* (2nd ed.). New York, NY: Wiley.

Fulleborn, A., & Meier, M. (1999). *SEM-business information collector at a glance.* SAP AG.

Garcia-Molina, H., Ullman, J. D., & Widom, J. (1999). *Database systems implementation.* Upper Saddle River, NJ: Prentice Hall.

Garcia-Molina, H., Ullman, J. D., & Widom, J. (2008). *Database systems: The complete book* (2nd ed.). Upper Saddle River, NJ: Prentice Hall.

Gartner Research. (2003). *Business intelligence tools: Perspective.* ID Number DPRO-93784.

Gemmell, J., Bell, G., & Lueder, R. (2006). MyLifeBits: A personal database for everything. *Communications of the ACM, 49*(1), 88–95.

Giarratano, J. C., & Riley, G. D. (2004). *Expert systems: Principles and programming* (4th ed.). Course Technology.

Hammer, M., & Champy, J. (2003). *Reengineering the corporation: A manifesto for business revolution.* New York, NY: Harper Paperbacks.

Han, J., & Kamber, M. (2006). *Data mining: Concepts and techniques* (2nd ed.). San Francisco, CA: Morgan Kaufmann.

Hand, D. J., Mannila, H., & Smyth, P. (2001). *Principles of data mining : Adaptive computation and machine learning.* Cambridge, MA: MIT Press.

Hartigan, J., & Wong, M. A. (1979). *K*-means clustering algorithm. *Applied Statistics, 28*(1), 100–108.

Hertz, J. A., Krogh, A. S., & Palmer, R. G. (1991). *Introduction to the theory of neural computation.* Boulder, CO: Westview Press.

Inmon, W. H. (2005). *Building the data warehouse* (4th ed.). New York, NY: Wiley.

Johnson, G., Scholes, K., & Whittington, R. (2008). *Exploring corporate strategy: Text and cases* (8th ed.). Englewood Cliffs, NJ: Prentice-Hall.

Kaplan, R. S., & Norton, D. P. (1996). *The balanced scorecard: Translating strategy into action.* Boston, MA: Harvard Business School Press.

Kaplan, R. S., & Norton, D. P. (2004). *Strategy maps: Converting intangible assets into tangible outcomes.* Boston, MA: Harvard Business School Press.

Kelly, S. (2006). *Customer intelligence: From data to dialogue.* New York, NY: Wiley.

Kimball, R., & Ross, M. (2002). *The data warehouse toolkit: The complete guide to dimensional modeling* (2nd ed.). New York, NY: Wiley.

Kisielnicki, J. (2008). *MIS—systemy informatyczne zarzadzania*. Warsaw, Poland: Placet.

Larose, D. T. (2004). *Discovering knowledge in data: An introduction to data mining*. New York, NY: Wiley.

Lawrence, D. (1999). *The economic value of information*. Berlin, Germany: Springer Verlag.

Linoff, G., & Berry, M. (2002). *Mining the web: Transforming customer data into customer value*. New York, NY: Wiley.

Luhn, H. P. (1958, October). A business intelligence system. *IBM Journal*.

MacQueen, J. (1967). Some methods for classifications and analysis for multivariate observations. *Proceedings of the 5th Berkeley Symposium on Mathematical Statistics and Probability, 1*, 281–297.

Michalewicz, Z. (1996). *Genetic algorithms + data structure = evolution programs*. Berlin, Germany: Springer Verlag.

Mitchell, T. M. (1997). *Machine learning*. New York, NY: McGraw-Hill.

Nash, E. (2000). *Direct marketing: Strategy, planning, execution* (4th ed.). New York, NY: McGraw-Hill.

Newell, A., & Simon, H. (1972). *Human problem solving*. New York, NY: Prentice Hall.

Obłój, K. (2007). *Strategia organizacji: W poszukiwaniu trwałej przewagi konkurencyjnej*. Warsaw, Poland: PWE.

O'Donnell, P., Arnott, D., & Gibson, G. (2002). *Data warehousing development methodologies: A comparative analysis* (Working paper, no. 2002/02). Melbourne, Australia: Decision Support Systems Laboratory, Monash University.

Osterle, H., Winter, R., Back, A., & Brenner, W. (2004). *Business engineering: Die ersten 15 Jahre*. Berlin, Germany: Springer Verlag.

Paramenter, D. (2007). *Key performance indicators*. New York, NY: Wiley.

Piatetsky-Shapiro, G., Fayyad, U., Smyth, P., & Uthurusamy, R. (1996). *Advances in knowledge discovery and data mining*. Cambridge, MA: AAAI/MIT Press.

Popper, K. (2004). *The logic of scientific discovery* (2nd ed.). London, UK: Routledge.

Porter, M. E. (1998). *Competitive advantage: Creating and sustaining superior performance*. New York, NY: Free Press.

PROMET. (1997). *Business process redesign* (Technical Report, version 2.0. IMG).

Quinlan, J. (1993). *C4.5: Programs for machine learning*. San Francisco, CA: Morgan Kaufmann.

Rappaport, A. (1986). *Creating shareholder value: The new standard for business performance*. New York, NY: Free Press.

Reinschmidt, J., Gottschalk, H., Kim, H., & Zwieitering, D. (1999). *Intelligent miner for data: Enhance your business intelligence* (IBM Report SG24-5422-00).

Rószkiewicz, M. (2002). *Narzedzia statystyczne w analizach marketingowych*. Warsaw, Poland: C. H. Beck.

Rummler, G. A., & Brache, A. P. (1995). *Improving performance: How to manage the white space in the organization chart* (2nd ed.). San Francisco, CA: Jossey-Bass.

Russel, S., & Norvig, P. (2009). *Artificial intelligence: A modern approach* (3rd ed.). New York, NY: Prentice Hall.

SAS. (2000). *Rapid warehousing methodology*. SAS Institute.

Schall, L. D., & Haley, C. W. (1991). *Introduction to financial management* (6th ed.). New York, NY: McGraw-Hill.

Shapiro, C., & Varian, H. R. (1998). *Information rules: A strategic guide to the network economy*. Boston, MA: Harvard Business School Press.

Silverstone, L. (2001). *The data model resource book, vol. 1: A library of universal data models for all enterprises*. New York, NY: Wiley.

Simon, H. (1977). *The new science of management decision*. New York, NY: Prentice Hall.

Stefanowicz, B. (2007). *Informatyczne systemy zarz dzania—Przewodnik*. Warsaw, Poland: Szkoła Główna Handlowa.

Stoner, J. A., Freeman, R. E., & Gilbert, D. R. (1995). *Management* (6th ed.). New York, NY: Prentice Hall.

Surma, J. (2008). Supporting value based management by business intelligence. In A. Herman and A. Szablewski (Eds.), *Value creation in the era of service economy*. Warsaw, Poland: Warsaw School of Economics.

Surma, J., & Furmanek, A. (2010). Improving marketing response by data mining in social network. Paper presented at the 2nd International Conference on Mining Social Networks for Decision Support, Odense, Denmark.

Thurow, L. (1991). Foreword. In M. S. S. Morton (Ed.), *The corporation of the 1990s: Information technology and organizational transformation*. Oxford, UK: Oxford University Press.

Todman, C. (2001). *Designing a data warehouse: Supporting customer relationship management*. New York, NY: Prentice Hall.

Turner, M. (1998). Expert systems and decision support. *Expert Systems for Information Management*, *1*, 3–21.

Tyson, K. W. (2002). *The complete guide to competitive intelligence* (2nd ed.). Kirk Tyson International, Ltd.

Ullman, J. D., & Widom, J. (2007). *First course in database systems* (3rd ed.). New York, NY: Prentice Hall.

US Fair Trade Commission. (2000, May 15). *Report of the advisory committee of the US Fair Trade Commission on online security and access*. Washington, DC: Author.

Wasserman, S., & Faust, K. (2009). *Social network analysis: Methods and applications*. Cambridge, UK: Cambridge University Press.

Weil, P., & Broadbent, M. (1998). *Leveraging the new infrastructure.* Boston, MA: Harvard Business School Press.

Weiss, S., & Kulikowski, C. (1991). *Computer systems that learn: Classification and prediction methods from statistics, neural networks, machine learning, and expert systems.* San Francisco, CA: Morgan Kaufmann.

Westerman, P. (2000). *Data warehousing: Using the Wal-Mart model.* San Francisco, CA: Morgan Kaufmann.

Williams, S., & Williams, N. (2003, Fall). The business value of business intelligence. *Business Intelligence Journal, 8*(4), 30–39.

Williams, S., & Williams, N. (2006). *The profit impact of business intelligence.* San Francisco, CA: Morgan Kaufmann.

Wrembel, R., Bebel, B., & Zadrozna, A. (2004). *Implementacja hurtowni danych—zagadnienia technologiczne. Konferencja Hurtownie Danych i Business Intelligence,* Warsaw, Poland.

Yang, J. (2008). *Clustering I—EECS 435* (PowerPoint presentation). Case-Western University. http://vorlon.case.edu/~jiong/cs435_2008/index.html

Index

Note: *f* indicates figure; *t* indicates table.

Announcing the Business Expert Press Digital Library

Concise E-books Business Students Need for Classroom and Research

This book can also be purchased in an e-book collection by your library as

- a one-time purchase,
- that is owned forever,
- allows for simultaneous readers,
- has no restrictions on printing, and
- can be downloaded as PDFs from within the library community.

Our digital library collections are a great solution to beat the rising cost of textbooks. e-books can be loaded into their course management systems or onto student's e-book readers.

The BUSINESS EXPERT PRESS digital libraries are very affordable, with no obligation to buy in future years.

For more information, please visit WWW.BUSINESSEXPERT.COM/LIBRARIES. To set up a trial in the United States, please contact SHERI ALLEN at *sheri.allen@globalepress.com*; for all other regions, contact NICOLE LEE at **NICOLE.LEE@IGROUPNET.COM**.

STRATEGIC MANAGEMENT
Series Editor: Mason Carpenter

An Executive's Primer on the Strategy of Social Networks by Mason Carpenter

Building Strategy and Performance Through Time: The Critical Path by Kim Warren

Knowledge Management: Begging for a Bigger Role 2e by Arnold Kransdorff

Sustainable Business: An Executive's Primer by Nancy Landrum and Sally Edwards

Mergers and Acquisitions: Turmoil in Top Management Teams by Jeffrey Krug

Positive Management: Increasing Employee Productivity by Jack Walters

A Leader's Guide to Knowledge Management: Drawing on the Past to Enhance Future Performance by John Girard and JoAnn Girard

Fundamentals of Global Strategy: A Business Model Approach by Cornelis de Kluyver

Operational Leadership by Andrew Spanyi

Succeeding at the Top: A Self-Paced Workbook for Newly Appointed CEOs and Executives by Bernard Liebowitz

Achieving Excellence in Management: Identifying and Learning from Bad Practices by Andrew Kilner

Dynamic Strategies for Small Businesses by Sviatoslav Steve Seteroff and Lydia Guadalupe Campuzano

Strategic Analysis and Choice: A Structured Approach by Alfred G. Warner